Joseph Cornish

A Serious and Earnest Address to Protestant Dissenters

representing the many and important principles, on which their dissent

from the Establishment is grounded

Joseph Cornish

A Serious and Earnest Address to Protestant Dissenters
representing the many and important principles, on which their dissent from the Establishment is grounded

ISBN/EAN: 9783337192693

Printed in Europe, USA, Canada, Australia, Japan

Cover: Foto ©Lupo / pixelio.de

More available books at **www.hansebooks.com**

A
Serious and earneſt Addreſs

TO

PROTESTANT DISSENTERS

REPRESENTING

The many and important Principles, on which their Diſſent from the ESTABLISHMENT is grounded.

My kingdom is not of this world, John xviii. 36.

One is your maſter even Chriſt, Matt. xxiii. 8.

▆▆ therefore in the liberty wherewith Chriſt hath ▆▆ free, and be not entangled again with the yoke of bondage. For brethren, ye have been called unto liberty, Galat. v. 1, 12.

LONDON.

Printed for J. JOHNSON, No. 72, St. Paul's Church Yard.
MDCCLXXII.

A

SERIOUS ADDRESS, &c.

Brethren, Fellow-Christians, and Protestant Dissenters,

I DO not pretend by this address, to offer any new arguments in favour of our dissent from the established church. So many excellent pieces have been written on this subject, that it would be the highest degree of vanity to attempt it. My design is to draw up the reasons urged by other writers into a small compass, and sell the piece at so low a price, that, not only the poorer sort may be able to purchase it, but others who have a regard to our interest, may be disposed to distribute them. A favour which I can ask with a good grace since no one can suspect, that the expectation of profit should induce me to publish a threepenny pamphlet. To set the argument in a strong clear light is my aim, but God is my witness, to whom I must give an account as well for what I write, as what I say; that not one single circumstance is designedly misrepresented or aggravated; if therefore, I have been in any respect mistaken, I am open to conviction, yet if the greater part, or even but a few of the arguments here offered are unexceptionable, every person must then judge for himself with regard to their strength and importance. However, I am not afraid to let them pass under the severest inspection of the most critical eye; not being conscious of having advanced one single objection

which

which the eftablifhed church is not juftly liable to. The principles of our diffent are fo well grounded, our reafons for it fo many and important, that I am very certain were they better known, efpecially to the younger fort, we fhould never decline fo faft. I pray God, this humble attempt may ftir up in the prefent and the rifing generation, a regard for that intereft, in defence of which fo many and fuch excellent characters have fuffered the lofs of all things and even life itfelf.

Our anceftors the Puritans, having been moft unjuftly reprefented by the greateft part of our hiftorians as a fet of weak enthufiafts, and by many as a race of hypocrites: I had drawn up a fhort account of them with an intention to publifh it in this addrefs, but finding it could not be done without enhancing the price, with fome reluctance I declined it; fhould this attempt however meet with encouragement, it may probably come out as a fupplement to it.

Objections were made to the eftablifhed forms, in the very infancy of the reformation, even in the time of Edward VI. and that by fome of the greateft and beft of the reformers, who died martyrs to the caufe. The Nonconformifts through the reigns of queen Elizabeth, James I. and Charles I. were very numerous, eminent for their piety and learning, and no lefs fo for their fufferings from the bifhops and fpiritual courts. In the reign of Charles I. the attacks made on the civil and religious liberties of the people were fo intolerable, that they firft of all abolifhed epifcopacy, and then monarchy itfelf. The prefbyterians have been frequently but moft falfely charged with the death of Charles I. but the perfons who accufe them are either very ignorant or very partial, for their minifters remonftrated againft it in the ftrongeft terms, and fuffered much in the royal caufe. That deed was committed by a fet of men who were not fo much of any one religious fect as a mixture of all. The prefbyterians were very warm in the reftoration of Charles II. as he himfelf acknowledged in his declarations, and made them large promifes; but thefe were all broken. No fooner was the king well fixed on the throne, than an act of uniformity was paffed, which the minifters fcrupling to comply with, on Bartholomew

day

day, Auguſt 24, 1662. near two thouſand of them were
turned out of their preferments in the church, to naked-
neſs and famine, and harraſſed by other oppreſſive acts,
ſo that many of them died in the common priſons.
That they were men of learning, piety, and the moſt
extenſive uſefulneſs none can deny; of their ſincerity
they afforded ſufficient proof in having endured ſo much,
for the teſtimony of a good conſcience. Numbers of
the laity, ſtood firm to their faithful paſtors in theſe
trying times, and when the glorious king William put
an end to theſe cruel perſecutions, it appeared, that no
leſs than ſixty thouſand perſons had ſuffered on a religious account, from the reſtoration of Charles II. to the
revolution of king William; five thouſand of whom
died in priſon. And beſide thoſe that ſuffered at home,
great numbers retired to the plantations of America
and fled to Holland, to the great detriment of their private affairs, and to trade in general. At a low com-
putation their loſſes amounted to twelve or fourteen
millions, a prodigious ſum for thoſe times. Nevertheleſs they were not diſcouraged, but ſtood up boldly for
the ſimplicity of the goſpel in oppoſition to the inventions of men, and not diſmayed by their afflictions,
contributed generouſly, when a liberty was given, to build
meeting houſes, and ſupport an intereſt for which they
had ſuffered ſo much. Let their poſterity conſider this.

In laying down the reaſons of our diſſent, it ſeems
natural to begin with the thirty-nine articles.

The clergy are not only obliged to ſubſcribe thirty-
nine articles drawn up by fallible men; but upon their
induction into any living muſt read them over, before
the whole congregation, and muſt likewiſe call God to
witneſs, to the ſincerity and truth with which they ſubſcribe them. This, biſhop Burnet calls a great impoſi-
tion, and it has been a very heavy burden to many
worthy men ſince his time, and is ſo even now, as appears from a deſign on foot of preſenting a petition to
deliver them from this yoke. I heartily wiſh them ſucceſs, if they fail in their attempt, that they may be ani-
mated with the ſame chriſtian fortitude and zeal for
truth, which led our illuſtrious two thouſand miniſters
(near that number) to leave their preferments in the

A 3   church,

church, and expofe themfelves to fharp afflictions, for
the teftimony of a good confcience and as a proof of
their fincerity; of which they had a noble example not
long ago, in a worthy clergyman of Ireland, who when
he had confidered the matter, refigned a living of one
hundred and fifty pound per annum, and refufed another
of equal value, which he might have held together with
it. It reflects fome difhonour on us diffenters, that this
Ifraelite indeed has not been taken greater notice of.
If I am rightly informed, he keeps a fchool at prefent,
fomewhere in Northamptonfhire for the fupport of his
family.

Whether or not, the articles are agreeable to fcripture
is not at prefent the queftion, (this however is certain,
that they are conftantly fubfcribed by perfons, whofe
fentiments are as contrary to one another, as light and
darknefs; a circumftance which has occafioned mutual
upbraidings) but, what authority is there in the word
of God for demanding fuch a teft, and what end does it anfwer? The only confeffion required or given in fcripture, is that of faith in the lord Jefus Chrift; and when
our bleffed faviour afked his difciples, whom fay ye
that I am? Simon Peter, anfwered and faid, thou art
Chrift, the fon of the living God. *Mat.* xvi. 15, 16.
with which he was fo well pleafed, that he immediately
gave him that gracious promife; thou art Peter, and
upon this rock I will build my church, and the gates
of hell fhall not prevail againft it. And I will give
unto thee, the keys of the kingdom of heaven. This
was verified by the fuccefs of St. Peter's fermons, *Acts* ii.
whereby three thoufand fouls were converted, and the
foundation of the firft chriftian church laid, and the
door of the kingdom of heaven, that is the gofpel difpenfation, as this phrafe commonly fignifies in the new
teftament, was opened. The exhortations given to try
the fpirits, to fpeak the words which become found
doctrine, and other texts relating to the minifters, by no
means imply that fuch confeffions were demanded; neither is there any precept to future times with regard to
this matter, which was it of fo great importance as has
been reprefented, would have been at leaft hinted at, efpecially by St. Paul, who folemnly declares to the elders

ders of the church of Ephesus, that he kept back nothing that was profitable, *Acts* xx. 20. And that he had shewed them all things v. 35. which must certainly mean every thing necessary to their present and future welfare as a church. But if there is no ground for such an imposition in the scripture, there may it is said be strong arguments drawn from the utility of established confessions. It may be asked therefore, what end do they answer?

The reason given by the compilers, is set forth in their short preface to the articles, *ad tolendam opinionum dissentium, et consensum in vera religione firmandum*, i. e. literally, to take away difference of opinions, and to establish an agreement in true religion. But how any articles can effect this, is strange indeed. If men have made use of their reason in religious enquiries, and embraced any particular opinions as the result of such sober enquiry; can a set of articles set forth by ever so great an authority alter their notions of things, at once remove them from their settled judgment and bring them to an agreement with such a set of articles? to suppose it is the highest absurdity; it may produce a change in the outward profession, but not in the heart, and whether such a change is desireable, judge ye? such is the absurdity arising from the strict and literal sense. But to prevent diversity of opinions, may be a more favourable and is a more general construction; which must either mean to keep persons of a contrary opinion out of the church, else, as one of her last great champions Mr. White observes, every parish might have a system of divinity peculiar to itself, nay there might be divers in the same parish. " The doctor in the morning would " teach his people orthodoxy, and the afternoon " preacher give them a lecture of rank arianism. The " next lords day, a disciple of Socinus, get into the " pulpit, and twenty species besides of heretics and " enthusiasts, one after another". This evil which he has represented in so terrible a light, their subscriptions have not prevented. It is not desirable by such means to prevent this diversity, there should be nothing to bias the mind of a christian, especially of a minister, he should be always open to free enquiry, and not dread to study the scriptures impartially, because it may lead him into sentiments different from the thirty-nine articles, thus making them sit heavy on his mind, and lead him to make pitiful evasions; which will be the case with many honest men, since after all their studies and labours, without this they are undone : for it is the language of the church, subscribe or starve.

The most that can be expected, is a unity of sounds in the bonds of ignorance, or a unity of practice in the bonds of hypocrisy; how despicable the one, how abominable the other ! But even such a union has by some been thought desirable, since the peace of the church, as they call it, may be thus in some measure preserved. But it has not effected even so much as this. For it is notorious,

That the doctrinal articles of the church are calvinistical, as even the most simple may see, who will read the 9, 11, 13, 17, and 18. Notwithstanding by far the most considerable part of the clergy, both for numbers and learning, are, and ever since the reign of Charles I. have been Arminians, and very zealous ones. To what sad shifts they have been put, to reconcile this subscription to, and solemn declaration, that they are agreeable to the word of God, with their avowed sentiments, is well known. Would to God, that for the honour of Christianity, the very remembrance of these evasions had perished, but while the evil continues, it is the duty of every one to expose it. Bishop Burnet, together with many more, plead that the articles are not so strictly worded, but that men of different sentiments may subscribe them, which is a flat contradiction to the declared intention, of preventing diversity of opinions; however they would fain make it out that they admit a latitude, and that this was probably intended by the compilers. This is contrary to fact.

All the Protestant divines of the church, whether Puritans or others, were of one mind, and esteemed them Calvinistical; 'till one Barret, in the year 1595, in a sermon preached before the university of Cambridge, declared against the Calvinistical doctrines of predestination and falling from grace; which was so offensive to the scholars, that they complained to archbishop

bishop Whitgift, and obtained nine articles, which were consented and subscribed to by several other bishops, to be sent down to the university, which the scholars were strictly enjoined to conform their judgments unto, and not to vary from. I am informed that all who take any degrees, are obliged to subscribe them to this day. They enforce the Calvinistical notions, by the strongest expressions language can admit. Not having room for all these, four may serve as a specimen.

I. That God from eternity has predestinated some persons to life, and reprobated others to death.

II. The moving or efficient cause of predestination to life, is not foreseen faith or good works, or any other commendable quality in the persons predestinated, but the good will and pleasure of God.

III. The number of the predestinate is fixed, and cannot be lessened or encreased.

VII. Saving grace is not communicated to all men ; neither have all men such a measure of divine assistance, that they may be saved if they will.

However, the Arminian doctrines gained ground, and others joined in explaining the articles in such a sense, as the church for twenty-five years after their being established by authority, and many more from their first compilation, never thought of.

It is likewise worthy to be remarked, that when bishop Burnet had published his laboured Exposition of the Thirty-nine Articles, about which he had taken so much pains, and which had been examined and approved by both the archbishops, several of the bishops, and a great many learned divines, (as he says in the preface), The design of which Exposition was to point out the only method of subscription, which would not expose a large majority of them to the reproach of prevarication,

Notwithstanding this seemed to him so necessary, and was so greatly approved by many, yet the lower house of convocation fell upon it with the utmost fury, as a performance full of scandal to the church, and danger to religion, and employed one, in the name of the rest, to write against it, which was accordingly done.

The

The writer's defign was to fhew, that the article
were framed to prevent diverfities of opinions, and h
endeavoured to prove they had done fo. Thefe inftance
feem to fhew, that no latitude can be admitted, without contradicting their defign, and rendering them ufe-
lefs.

Some fay, that they fubfcribe them as articles of
peace ; but they are articles of faith, to be believed,
not merely acquiefced in, and folemnly fubfcribed, as
agreeable to the word of God. Some would have had
bifhop Burnet to have explained them in that manner ;
but judge Burnet, his fon, obferves, " that there might
" perhaps be reafon to wifh, that they had only been
" impofed as fuch, but there was nothing in our con-
" ftitution to warrant an expofitor in giving that fenfe
" to them."

Others talk of fubfcribing them as far as they are
agreeable to the fcripture, but as this will not anfwer
the defign of the church, fo by the fame evafion they
might fubfcribe a Popifh creed, or the Koran of Mahomet. They muft declare that they are, not fubfcribed them as far as they are, agreeable to the word
of God.

Who can read the Athanafian creed, together with
the firft, fecond, fifth, and eighth articles, without being
convinced, that they are defigned to keep out all op-
pofers of the Trinity ; yet the notions both of Arius
and Socinus are imbibed by numbers of the clergy ; and
an ingenious member of that body has lately endeavoured to prove, that fuch may confcientioufly fubfcribe.
It is eafy to obferve what their boafted unity comes
to.

. No articles can be fo ftrictly worded, but that bad
men, for the fake of preferment, will fubfcribe to them ;
others will ftrain their confciences for the fake of thefe
emoluments, or to get a fubfiftence, which after they
have fpent much time and money in their education,
they cannot procure by any other means. This muft
expofe the miniftry and religion itfelf to contempt, and
after all none be kept out of the church by thefe means,
but honeft, upright men, who will not for the fake of
worldly advantages, make fhipwreck of a good confcience

cience. Bleſſed be God there have been, and are ſuch who thus ſupport the cauſe of truth ; otherwiſe, between Popery on the one hand, and Deiſm on the other, true goſpel Chriſtianity would in theſe kingdoms be at a very low ebb.

Let Proteſtant Diſſenters act conſiſtently with their principles on this great point, never require aſſent to man-made propoſitions, but to the Bible only. Let the church of Rome, and other churches which claim authority in controverſies of faith, do as they pleaſe ; we ought to remember, that it is our grand principle, both as Proteſtants and Proteſtant Diſſenters, that the ſcripture is a ſufficient rule, independant of every other.

The confeſſions of faith uſually given by our miniſters at their ordinations, have been objected to us by the champions of the church. To this it is anſwered, Theſe confeſſions are voluntary ; they are not impoſed by any ſet of men, but drawn up by themſelves, and if delivered in the expreſs words of ſcripture, will in general (as indeed they ought) give ſatisfaction. However if any miniſter ſhould ſcruple to give in ſuch a confeſſion, which not one in a hundred would do, according to our preſent cuſtom, no reaſonable objection can be made to its being omitted, ſince the eaſieſt way to judge of the ſoundneſs of a miniſter's faith, is from his preaching and behaviour, and theſe are likewiſe ſufficient ſecurity. For if any man, who does not believe the great doctrines of revelation, will nevertheleſs for the ſake of a good ſalary, conduct the ſervice of a Chriſtian church, he would likewiſe give in any confeſſion whatever, which would contribute to his profit. Ordination confeſſions, ſhould and in general are conſidered as voluntary, for the ſatisfaction of the people, not neceſſary to an admittance into the miniſtry ; in which reſpect a little reflection will convince us, that they are of no ſervice at all. Some, therefore, have been ordained without any confeſſion, and that of a miniſter, who taking the Greek teſtament into his hand, ſaid, " This I believe to be the word of God, " the rule of faith and practice to Chriſtians ; as ſuch, " I ſhall endeavour to underſtand the true ſenſe of it, to
" incul-

" inculcate the genuine truths and duties of it, and to
" live according to it," was a good confeffion.

It ought, however, to be remembered, that by law,
fubfcription is required of Diffenting minifters, as well
as clergymen, to all the articles except three and half.
Our pious anceftors did not object to this, for when
the Proteftants firft broke off from the church of Rome,
many fects ftarted up, with which their adverfaries re-
proached them, faying, now they had left their church,
they knew not where to ftop, but would yield up all
the articles of the Chriftian faith. To avoid this the
wifer way would have been to have pleaded the fuf-
ficiency of fcripture, as they have fince done; but however particular churches drew up confeffions, and altered
them as they faw further into the truth. That of the
Dutch church was altered fixteen times, till finally
fettled by the fynod of Dort; and the articles of the
church of England were originally forty-two, but three
were afterwards left out, and alterations made in others,
which practice might have been continued had not their
hands been tied up. The Nonconformifts, therefore,
of the laft age, were not averfe to this practice; yet
though the law continues in force, fcarce any Diffenting
minifters now living, have fubfcribed, nor could many
in confcience do it if called upon. The civil government preferves us from ecclefiaftical vengeance on this
head; fo that when a great bifhop, fome years fince,
threatened to enquire into this matter, the minifters
bid him defiance; and there are few now of learning
and note, who would give up their Chriftian liberty in
this point. And as diffenting minifters oppofe thefe
unchriftian impofitions, when it is out of their power
to obtain the preferments annexed to them, this may
ferve to refute what fome have advanced, that take
away the emoluments and objections to fubfcriptions
would ceafe: they oppofe them on the firm bafis of
Chriftian liberty.

The articles, from fubfcribing to which the law itfelf frees us, fhall be briefly confidered; and it is left
to every one to determine concerning their importance
and weight. They are the 34th, 35th, 36th, and the
firft claufe of the 20th.

The

The 35th respects the homilies, setting forth that they contain a godly and wholesome doctrine, and neceffary for the times.

Thefe were compofed in the reign of Edward VI. and ufed inftead of fermons, the clergy being at that time fo ignorant, as to render this help neceffary: That they contain a godly and wholefome doctrine for the moft part, may not be difputed; but to give an unlimited approbation to a whole folio book of merely human compofition, (" and in which, upon that ac-
" count, as Dr. Bennet, an advocate for the church,
" obferves, it would be a miracle if nothing were
" really amifs, or what an honeft man might with a
" very good confcience diffent from") is unreafon-able.

Article 36, concerns the confecration of bifhops and minifters; and affirms, that the book of confecration of archbifhops aud bifhops, and ordering of priefts and deacons, doth contain all things neceffary to the confecration and ordering; neither hath it any thing that of itfelf is fuperftitious and ungodly.

That this book contains all things neceffary to the confecrating and ordering bifhops and minifters in the church of England, no one will deny. That there are fome parts fuperftitious, if not ungodly, feems clear. The bifhop elect, at his confecration, is to be prefented by two bifhops, to the arch-bifhop of the province in this form. " Moft reverend father in God, we prefent unto you, this godly and well learned man, to be or-dained and confecrated bifhop." Is it not fomewhat fuperftitious, that two bifhops muft prefent him, and that to an officer in the church, called an arch-bifhop, an officer never once mentioned in the New Teftament, any more than the reft of the ceremony, and to make any thing neceffary, in fuch folemnities, without au-thority derived from thence is fuperftitious. To call this bifhop elect a godly and well learned man, is, fometimes an ungodly action, fince 'tis to be feared that fome have been confecrated to this office, with but a little learning, and le's godlinefs.

Again, in the faid form of confecration, the arch-bifhop fays to the bifhop, Receive the Holy Ghoft for

the

the office and work of a bishop, in the church of God, now committed unto thee, by the imposition of our hands, and remember that thou stir up the grace of God, which is given thee by the imposition of our hands. How the Holy Ghost, and the grace of God, these great gifts, can be imparted by the imposition of their hands, who, if we may judge from their fruits, have neither, (since bishops are not always blameless) we cannot divine.

This is a very high, not to say, a presumptuous claim, without sufficient, if any warrant, from the word of God. It was a power indeed given to the apostles, that on whomsoever they laid their hands, the Holy Ghost should be given, Acts viii. 18. but it no where appears that they did or could leave these gifts to their successors. But, say they, we impart the ordinary gifts of the Holy Ghost as the apostles did the extraordinary gifts of the same Spirit. There is no such distinction made in the scripture, and therefore it may be enquired what is meant by it? The extraordinary, that is, the supernatural gifts, or miraculous powers, have ceased long since; these therefore the bishops do not pretend to confer. The weakness of such a pretence would indeed be evident to every one that could hear and see. If by the ordinary gifts, are meant the christian virtues, and good moral dispositions of heart, it by no means appears that these are conferred upon the person consecrated, or that they are indued with any qualities in which they were deficient before, if they are, let them shew it, and we will believe them. Similar to this, is the passage in the form of ordaining priests. Receive the Holy Ghost, for the office and work of a priest, in the church of God, now committed unto thee, by the imposition of our hands. Whose sins thou dost forgive, they are forgiven; and whose sins thou dost retain, they are retained. This however will be considered more largely hereafter, just observing here, that this amazing power, which the bishops of the church of England assume, is as high above the power of the kings and emperors of the world, as the heavens are above the earth, the power of investing every priest whom they ordain with a power to forgive and retain sins. Christ
gave

gave this power to his apostles, who had likewise other miraculous endowments, which all ceased together, and the apostles never pretended to confer the power of retaining, &c. on any person whatever, never presumed to say, I pardon thee, or I absolve thee, neither does it appear that the commission extended farther than this, to publish the glad tidings of salvation, through Christ, to all the world; declaring, that whoever repented, and believed in him, their sins should be forgiven, and they should be saved. Neither can any thinking person believe, that every young stripling, who applies for ordination, is moved by the Holy Ghost, to take upon him the office of a deacon, this they solemnly declare, but when it is not the case, it is ungodly.

As for us, we pretend neither to confer or receive any additional powers at ordination, but disclaim it as enormous, it is dishonourable to God to suppose that he would make that necessary, which it would be any way possible for men to deny conferring. This they undoubtedly may. Ordaining protestant dissenting ministers is looked upon chiefly as a useful expedient, for keeping out unfit persons, and solemnly imploring the blessing of God upon the labours of the persons thus ordained, before which it is not the custom to administer either the Sacraments of the Lord's Supper or Baptism, though without doubt as soon as any church approves of and chuses them, they derive their commission from the New Testament, to perform all the offices of pastors. Imposition of hands was a ceremony used in antient times, when they prayed over any person, to distinguish that person from others, and being likewise an apostolical custom, 1 Tim. iv. 14. 2 Tim. i. 6. is retained by us, but would easily be dispensed with, should any one object to or scruple it, because, those gifts are ceased which used to be conveyed by it.

Art. 34. Concerns the traditions and ceremonies of the church, " setting forth, that whosoever, through his " private judgment, wilfully and openly doth pur- " posely break the traditions and ceremonies of the " church, which be not repugnant to the word of God, " and be ordained by common authority, ought to be " rebuked openly, that others may fear to do the like."

We approve of the claufe, which be not repugnant to the word of God, but at the fame time affirm, that it is not lawful to introduce any ceremonies whatever, at leaft, to make them neceffary terms of communion. If the church of England has this right, fo has the church of Rome, and therefore according to their own article, whofoever fhall in a Popifh country, through his private judgment, break their traditions and ceremonies, through non compliance with them, fhall be rebuked openly, and this rebuke muft be fomewhat fevere, or it will not anfwer the end affigned, that others alfo may fear, on this plan therefore they may continue to the end of the world. The laft claufe of this article, allows, that every particular or national church, hath authority to ordain, change and abolifh ceremonies or rites of the church, ordained only by authority, fo that all things be done to edifying. That it has authority to abolifh them, we acknowledge, becaufe by rejecting the inventions of men, we fhall approach nearer to the fimplicity of the gofpel. It is even allowed on all hands, that the ceremonies enjoined in fcripture may be fet afide, when by a change of cuftoms and manners, they lofe their fignificancy. Wafhing one another feet was exprefly appointed by Chrift, and mentioned by the apoftles as a virtuous act, 1 Tim. v. 10. being a mark of true humility. It fhould be obferved, that in thefe warm countries, they only wore fandals, which fcarce came up to the mid-leg, it was therefore a ufual mark of civility fhewn to a ftranger, on entering the houfe, for a fervant to attend with water, wafhing the feet, being a neceffary refrefhment, but in this country, it would not be efteemed civility, but officious and troublefome, we therefore are to fhew our humility by actions at prefent more fignificant. So the kifs of charity, being the ufual method of falutation then, was proper, but in this country, to fee men kifs each other, would be ridiculous and difguftful. An order of deaconeffes was likewife appointed, Rom. xvi. 8. (that is the proper meaning of the word fervant,) but when this was made an occafion of

reproach

reproach it ceased.* However we cannot allow, the ordaining rites by man's authority, or even changing the old for others, so as to oblige others to an observancy of them; by such means the word of God might very soon, as of old, become void by their traditions, for it is the nature of ceremonies to eat out the vital part of religion, and as every new bishop or race of bishops would probably be for introducing something or other new, we should either be continually fluctuating, or else in time, have such a load as we should not be able to bear.

That clause of the 20th article, to which we object and are by law excused from subscribing, is as follows.

The church hath power to decree rites or ceremonies, and authority in controversies of faith.

This is similar to the former article, and worthy of particular consideration, since either would justify our dissent from the church, if we had no other objections to make. What is the church here spoken of? Never was a word used in a more vague, indeterminate sense, than this hath been by some writers, and that evidently to serve a turn; may we not however reasonably suppose, that it is used here in the same sense as in the article preceding it, i. e. the 19th, where it is defined thus:

"The visible church of Christ is a congregation of faithful men, in which the pure word of God is preached, and the sacraments be duly ministred, according to Christ's ordinance, in all those things that of necessity are requisite to the same."

What church? what congregation is this to whom this power and authority belong? where is it? who are the members of it? in what part of the world do they live? Does it mean the church of England, how can they prove it belongs to them any more than to the

---

* It does not follow from hence, that we may set aside the Lord's Supper, because we are expresly commanded thus to shew forth the Lord's death till he come, 2 Cor. ii. 26, or Baptism, both of which may be practised in any countries. Though if wine cannot be procured, any other liquor will serve as well, as will barley, rice, or oaten bread, instead of wheat, where the latter does not grow.

church

church of Scotland or of Ruffia? ought it not rather to exift in the church of Rome? we know they claimed it long before this church was eftablished or heard of (as to its prefent form) certainly they have as good a right to it, and therefore to reject what this venerable mother had eftablished, was on this principle wrong.

If it means every national church, according to the expreffion in the 34th article, how unjuftifiable is their conduct in cenfuring the national churches of France, Spain and Italy, for then they have this power likewife. Does it mean every particular congregation, which is apparently the true fenfe of the 19th article? What confufion would not this create, every fociety would have different ceremonies, all under the cover of authority, fo that 'tis poffible no two churches would be alike, and the inhabitants of one parish know not how to behave in the public worfhip of the next. Surely this would not be doing all things decently and in order. How far does this authority go? may they make three ceremonies? yes, the church of England has more, 10: what hinders, they may, like that of Rome, go on to a hundred, and there is nothing to forbid their encreafing to thoufands, it knows no bounds, but an arbitrary power is there claimed. Over whom does it extend? is it over their own members only, or may it, as was formerly the cafe, force others to compliance? Thefe are very important queftions, but it would be difficult to anfwer them to the fatisfaction of any reafonable man.

For any church whatever to lay claim to this power, is a bold ufurpation upon the office of Chrift, the only king in his church, it is to make the body the head, fince fuch a power belongs only to the head, which is Chrift; he hath appointed two rites in his church, and who hath power to introduce a third? Let thofe who lay claim to fuch a power, prove it from fome text of fcripture, clear, exprefs, and full to the purpofe: whoever without this claims fuch authority over their fellow chriftians, are not fubject to Chrift, but encroachers upon his province, and ufurp an authority which belongs to him only. It is not to be imagined that Chrift who came into this world, to fet up and eftablish a fpiritual kingdom,

dom, would leave it to weak and fallible men, to draw out the scheme or settle the form of it, or to vary and alter it according to their own humours and fancies to the end of the world. The laws and ordinances of his kingdom are all left upon record in the New Testament, by these only should every true christian be governed in things pertaining to the kingdom of God, and rejecting all human authority whatever in matters of religion, regard that, and that only as his rule.

And as to authority in matters of faith (in some copies of the articles, controversies of faith) does it imply an authority to make more articles of faith than are contained in the gospel? If so, these additional articles are either necessary to salvation, or they are not. To say *they are necessary, would contradict the scriptures,* in which are contained all things that pertain to life and godliness, 2 Pet. i. 3. it is to make the christian rule a very defective and altogether insufficient rule of faith. If they are not necessary to salvation, what good purpose doth this authority serve, what valuable end doth it answer? But, if the meaning be, that the church hath authority to interpret the rule of faith, and to force its interpretation on those who are subject to its authority, to make this good it must be first proved that the church is infallible, to this no church but that of Rome pretends, and therefore it may claim such an authority with a tolerable grace, but for a church which confesses herself fallible to claim what can only belong to infallibility, is not meerly strange, it is absurd and ridiculous. One of these it must mean, or this, that if it should put a wrong interpretation, it hath still power to enforce it.

What protestant will maintain either of these? What papist that will not make a handle of it, to defend all the superstitions of their church? What deist, who will not be led to despise the religion itself, when the ministers and professors of it claim powers, so destructive to the common rights, and so contrary to the common sense of mankind?

Indeed it is said, in the next clause of the article. " It is not lawful for the church to ordain any thing " that is contrary to God's word written, neither may
" it

" it so expound one place of scripture, that it be re-
" pugnant to another."

But who is to judge of this? If the persons over
whom this authority is claimed, it then comes to nothing, seeing they may either receive or reject it, but
if the church is to judge of this, then here is at once
established an implicit faith, in the church, that great
principle of popery. And this is the case, for when
once a doctrine is declared by the church to be agreeable to the word of God, what end will it answer, for
any person or persons to contradict it, for if it has authority in matters of faith, it must mean either to make
new articles, or to settle disputed points.

Now such a claim is weak and groundless; the apostles were endued with power from on high, and taught
by the peculiar inspiration of the spirit, but they never
claimed or exercised such an authority, they decreed no
rites or ceremonies as necessary to be used in christian
worship, but what Christ had instituted before he ascend-
ed to the Father. They did not require an implicit
faith, but reasoned out of the scriptures, and commend-
ed the persons as noble, not because they submitted to
their authority, but searched the scriptures daily, whether these things were so. Acts xvii. 2d and 11th verse.
After the Jews and Gentiles were converted to christianity, and submitted to the doctrine preached by the
apostles, so far from claiming, they expressly tell them,
that they have no dominion over their faith, 2 Cor. i. 24.
when the apostle Paul gives the Corinthians some necessary advice, though divinely inspired, so far from
demanding a consent on his bare word, he tells them,
I speak as to wise men, judge ye what I say, 2 Cor.
x. 15.

In the first general council, held by the apostles at
Jerusalem, they would lay no greater burden than such
things as appeared necessary to the Holy Ghost, and to
them who were inspired by him, Acts xv. Such as
were absolutely necessary to the welfare of christianity
then, but (except fornication, which was contrary to
the law of nature, but very common among the Gentiles) were not afterwards obligatory, as appears from
St. Paul's reasoning, 1 Cor. x. verse 22d to the end,
where

where we find eating things offered to idols, and consequently the other things forbidden were only to be avoided when they were an offence to any weak brother.

This claim then is not only groundless, having no foundation in scripture, but it is highly presumptuous and arrogant, and we may add, it is hurtful and dangerous. It has been the door to all the corruptions of the church of Rome, and it is by this authority, that so many kingdoms have been enslaved, and spiritual tyranny established throughout christendom. The slaughter and bloodshed, the havock and desolation occasioned by it is shocking. Emperors, kings, and princes, have been by this set on to murder and butcher their own subjects, or to carry fire and sword into the territories of their neighbours, who have gloriously stood up in defence of that liberty with which Christ hath made free, in opposition to this usurped authority, which we see is still claimed, tho', blessed be God, the exercise of it is in a great measure restrained. Owing to this were the persecutions which our brave forefathers the puritans endured for more than a century. It was this that lighted up the fires in the reign of bloody queen Mary. It was this that led on Lewis XIV. that execrable man, to persecute with such wanton cruelty his protestant subjects. This occasioned the massacre in Ireland in 1641, when 40,000 protestants were butchered and murdered, without distinction of age, sex, or condition; and that of Paris in 1572, when 10,000 were murdered in one night, and 20,000 more within the space of a few weeks, both lords and peasants, the hoary head, and infants at the breast. This gave rise and support to the inquisition. The time would fail to relate the horrid mischiefs with which church authority is chargeable ; suffice it to say, it was this which nailed Jesus to the tree. *The chief priests and elders of the people took counsel against Jesus, to put him to death,* Mat. xxvii. 1. and when the civil government would have released him, it was the chief priests and elders persuaded the people that they should ask Barabbas, and execute Jesus, ver. 20. John xviii. 40.

Authority has often consecrated error, nursed ignorance, and suppressed truth. Authority has made knaves: Authority has made fools: But mere authority has very feldom propagated virtue or true religion, nay it is abfolutely repugnant to the interest of both. The very claim of this authority is a reproach to Chriftianity, and an infult upon common fenfe. For Chrift's kingdom is not of this world; it was not fet up by any temporal power, nor is it to be fupported after the manner of earthly kingdoms, by temporal fanctions, but by fuch as are future, fpiritual, and invifible.

As long then as the church of England lays claim to this authority, and requires all her minifters to affent to it, and her members to fubmit to it, it will be a hard matter to vindicate herfelf againft, and very unreafonable to cenfue, the errors and fuperftitions of the church of Rome, fince that church can lay claim to authority with at leaft as good a grace, and they think better. Should every thing elfe therefore be altered to which we object, yet unlefs this bold claim is given up, our allegiance to Chrift, the only King in his church, juftifies, yea obliges us to diffent from it.

It is proper to obferve, that fubfcription to the thirty-nine articles is not only required of thofe who enter on the miniftry, but of every ftudent who enters himfelf at any college in the univerfities. But how abfurd and unreafonable to demand this of young perfons juft come from a grammar-fchool, who in general know nothing about the matter, and confidering how much they have been debated among the moft learned and experienced men, it cannot be expected that fuch fhould be qualified to fubfcribe them. This method, however, fills them with early prejudices, and being brought fo foon under the yoke, it does not fit fo eafy as fuperior knowledge and difcernment might make it. One, if not more, of the colleges at Cambridge have dropt this practice, an example worthy to be followed by every feminary.

As the church claims an authority as to appointing ceremonies, fo it enjoins fome on its members, to which the diffenters have always objected.

1. Kneeling at the facrament. That our Lord and his apoftles celebrated this rite in the common table pofture of that country, is in general if not univerfally
agreed,

agreed, it feems natural therefore that we fhould ufe the pofture common to us. Kneeling, however, has been efteemed by many a more decent and devout pofture ; fuch would do well to confider, that it is at leaft probable, that this cuftom firft took its rife, when the abfurd and monftrous doctrine of tranfubftantiation was invented, and when men were fo fadly deluded, as to believe that a piece of bread was really converted into the very body, blood, and foul of Chrift, and that our Redeemer ftill continued to be offered up as a facrifice, exprefly contrary to the words of the apoftle to the Hebrews, fo often repeated, chap. ix. ver. 25, 26, 28. and chap. x. ver. 10, 12, 14. but as thefe horrid doctrines were rejected at the Reformation, when the fcriptures began to be read, many thought the kneeling pofture fhould be difcontinued, as a remnant of popifh idolatry. The church of England, however, continues this, and no perfon can be admitted to receive the Lord's fupper, without complying, except they fhould labour under fome natural defect, which does not happen once in a century. This is certainly an infringement on our Chriftian liberty, the pofture contributes nothing to the worthy receiving of it ; and as the fcriptures have left it indifferent, to impofe it is unreafonable, and to refufe fubmitting to it juftifiable. Sitting was the cuftom pleaded for by the puritans, yet they were willing to leave it to every ones judgment, either to ftand, fit, or kneel as they pleafed. Kneeling has been practifed by fome perfons in our different churches, and is to this day, none have objected to it, but every one is left to be fully fatisfied in his own mind. Had the church done this much, contention would have been avoided.

3. The fign of the crofs in baptifm, " in token (fays that office in the common prayer) " that hereafter the " child fhall not be afhamed to confefs the faith of " Chrift crucified." But however fignificant this ceremony may be, there is not the leaft trace of it in the Bible ; and why are not the fpittle and falt ufed by the papifts in this office, the firft put into the ear of the child, to denote that his ears fhall be open to the word of God, and the falt into his mouth, in remembrance

of

of Chrift's difciples being called the falt of the earth; full as fignificant ceremonies, or at leaft of equal authority, with the fign of the crofs. They were all found in the church of Rome, and why that of England fhould take the one and leave the two others no folid reafon can be affigned, and yet a child cannot be baptized in this proteftant church, without the application of this popifh relic. Sponfors in baptifm will be fpoken of hereafter.

3. Bowing at the name of Jefus, which is exprefly commanded by the eighteenth canon. The text Phil. ii. 10. That *at the name of Jefus every knee fhall bow*, it is acknowledged by the learned of the church doth not authorife or enjoin the practice; and Dr. Nichols, its great champion fays, " they are not fo dull as to think " that thofe words can be rigoroufly applied to this pur- " pofe." If they can, none but the women obey it, fince the men bow only their heads. There is then no fhadow of argument for it either from reafon or fcripture. And it feems ftrange, that this reverence fhould be made at the name of Jefus, which was common to other perfons, and not at Jehovah, God, Chrift, Meffiah, thefe peculiar epithets; who can account for this?

4. Bowing to the eaft, if not enjoined by any canon now in force, is univerfally practifed; but to what oriental deity is this worfhip given? not, furely, to the immenfe, omniprefent Jehovah? he is an infinite fpirit, and alike prefent in all places, this cuftom might lead weak men to falfe, unworthy notions of him. If it be faid the worfhip is paid toward the altar, this is worfhipping ftones or wood, for the prefence of God is not in one part of the church more than another, (though under the Jewifh difpenfation, his glories were more apparent over the ark) while the breaden God was upon it, thofe who believed it to be the very body of Chrift might do well to pay their homage to it, but now that idol is taken away, what divinity is there in the altar to demand religious homage?

5. The white furplice which the clergy are obliged to wear, is one of the popifh relicks. Our Saviour's appearing in bright raiment, as white as fnow, and the
angels

angels being generally said to have appeared in white, Acts i. 10. Mark xvi. 5. Jude iii. 4. &c. have been ridiculously urged in favour of this. Ridiculous, I say, for they might as well use some art to make their countenances shine, or be girt about the paps with a golden girdle, as Christ appeared to St. John, Rev i. 13. But they had better stay for this till they become like the angels of God, and appear in glory. And it would be more to their honour to imitate Christ in the humble, mean manner in which he ordinarily appeared, rather than as shining in glory. But it has been said, they ought not to administer the sacraments in the dress which they wear in the streets. Why not? Though under the Old Testament holy garments were prescribed by God, the New makes no difference in them; and if this argument holds good, they should change their other garments, particularly shoes, which contract most dirt. As to our wearing black, it is not that we attribute any thing to colour or cloth, neither is it imposed, other colours are used; gravity is proper even in dress, but gravity of conduct is most requisite in a minister. The band was formerly a part of dress common to all, and is not at present peculiar to ministers, being worn by councellors and others; and so far is it from being accounted necessary, that some wear it seldom, and others never. But to make any particular, especially an uncommon dress, absolutely necessary, as the surplice is, leads some to think that the ministerial character consists in the colour and shape of garments, it ought, however, to be considered as consisting in somewhat more important. About the richer attire of bishops and cathedral dignitaries I say nothing; but surely the cathedral service is liable to just exception, to maintain, at a great expence, a number of persons to sing and chant away the most solemn prayers, without the least appearance of devotion, or tendency to promote it in others, is at best useless, and to many must be very offensive.

6. The observation of saints days, and such a multitude of fasts and feasts as the church enjoins, so that one or other of them falls on more than half the days in the year, is without scripture-foundation; they are

C   now

now, 'tis true, but little regarded, except that collect
are appointed for particular seasons. To record any
great deliverance peculiar to our own country, as the
5th of November, &c. seems reasonable, otherwise
they may be forgot. For the gift of Christ, and the
blessings of the new covenant, God hath set apart one
day in seven, by observing which we shall do well. In
the observation of other seasons and days, the churche
of England and Rome exactly agree in time, and they
were appointed by the pope, not by the gospel. I
may be asked, What harm is there in these things.
Much. They are mere human inventions, never ap
pointed by Christ, who is alone our master, Mat. xxiii
8. nor by the apostles, whom he left to instruct; and
therefore. if innocent in themselves, cease to be so
when imposed by fallible 'men. Besides, if one ceremony is introduced, why not five, or ten, or an hundred?
Where shall we stop? Will it be pleaded that ceremonies and rites are different from fopperies and superstitions; it will be very hard to draw the line betwixt
them. Consecrating water to sprinkle the living, will
be deemed a popish foppery, but I would defy the
utmost art of man to shew that consecrating ground to
cover a dead body, (another decent ceremony of the
church, I had almost forgot) is less so; nor can any
one upon earth shew that salt and spittle in baptism are
less instructive than the sign of the cross. Consecrating
churches is an useless superstition, (especially in the
manner archbishop Laud was wont to do it) how is it
possible to convey holiness to stone walls? The word
church, in scripture, always means the people, not the
building, Mat. xviii. 17. Acts ii. 47 —v. 11.—viii. 1.
1 Cor. xiv. 4. &c. They met in private houses, Col. iv.
15. Philemon, ver. 2. and in times of persecution in
fields or woods. Dissenters build places for this purpose of meeting, without supposing any particular holiness in them, and take off their hats at entering on account of the people assembled. When divine service
is not performing, there is nothing more holy in a cathedral than a barn. When power is once given to
appoint rites according to the pleasure of men, there is
no knowing where it will stop. Things ridiculous and
absurd

abfurd will foon be introduced under the fpecious name
of decent ceremonies. When archbifhop Laud, fo
long the favourite of our high churchmen, was at the
head of it, lighted candles were put upon the altar,
copes were bought of mafs priefts, with crucifixes and
images of the trinity painted on them, confecrated
knives to cut the facramental bread, cannifters for
wafers lined with cambrick lace, and images of the
virgin Mary erected, undoubtedly intended to enliven
the beauties of holinefs in the church, and had it not
been for the heroic ftand which the puritans and their
fucceffors have made againft this rite-making fpirit, the
church of England might by this have fallen little fhort
in thefe additional fplendors of the church of Rome
itfelf. Such are the fruits of authority to decree rites
and ceremonies. Thofe who can approve them do well
to ufe them ; to impofe them on others is unchriftian,
but the church obliges us either to comply with what
we cannot approve, or to feparate. Very different was
the conduct of St. Paul, he preferred fuffering the
greateft inconvenience, fooner than offend his weak ·
brother, 1 Cor. viii. 13. and is very particular in ex-
horting to mutual forbearance with regard to thefe indifferent things, Rom. xiv. 1 Cor. x. 23. to the end.
But when the Jews would infift on the Gentiles conforming to the mofaic ritual, he would not give place
by fubjection to them, no not for an hour, Gal. ii. 5.
and he gives them a noble exhortation to ftand faft
in their Chriftian liberty, chap. vi. to ver. 15. Let us
remember the advice, and as the primitive Chriftians
were thus exhorted not to return to the yoke of Jewifh
ceremonies, fo let us oppofe all fuch encroachments,
and never be drawn into a compliance through a pretended antiquity ; for this impofing fpirit began very
early, fee Acts xv. and it is always the nature of human
inventions to deftroy the vital fpirit of religion, and
fwallow up true goodnefs in empty fhew and vain foppery ; but in whatever any church teaches for doctrines
the commandments of men, fo far we ought to withdraw
from it.

The liturgy or common prayer ufed in the church of
England, is another reafon for our diffent. There has

much faid lately for compofed forms of prayer, and fome
diffenters favour and ufe them. In particular cafes
they may be expedient, but free prayer, where minifters have fluency of fpeech and matter, feems moft
natural at leaft, and whatever may be objected to it, is
certainly conducted with great propriety in many of
our congregations. Young men, and fuch as are apt
to hefitate, may find it very ufeful to compofe their
prayers, and if it does not give offence to the people,
writing them down, occafionally may prevent confufion
and irregularity. But let this be as it may, our objections to the eftablifhed liturgy are many, and well-
grounded. There is no liberty given to minifters to
contract or alter it at any time whatever; in churches
which have prayers every day, there is juft the fame
form from week to week, from year to year, and fo
on for ever. There are indeed, collects for particular
days, but thefe are very fhort. Too much, or what is
often repeated, even of the beft things, is apt to tire;
but were three or four fervices appointed, or a liberty
given to the minifter to leave out a part, and introduce
one of his own compofing, it would make a variety,
and furely a perfon is hardly fit for the office, who cannot occafionally do this with propriety; indeed this
liberty is allowed in a prayer before fermon, but owing
to the length of the fervice, this generally is and had
need be very fhort; however this may obviate one filly
objection made againft free prayer, that men by this
means may introduce their own trifling affairs, and even
feditious matters in the public congregations. The beft
things to be fure may be abufed, but if men are fo
very prone to fuch faults, we fee even the church
leaves a door open for committing them.

If a diffenting minifter fhould always ufe the fame
prayer, the people will fometimes be relieved by hearing other minifters; but whatever minifter, or whatever
place our brethren of the eftablifhment are, it is always
the fame. If any fhould afk, how then can attention
be kept up in the Lord's prayer, it is anfwered, it is
but very fhort, and the thought of its being our Lord's
own form, gives its weight; but we by no means approve of the frequent repetition of it in the church-
ferviceervice;

service ; where, in the morning only of the Lord's day, it is used five times, if there be a communion seven times ; and by the intervention of the offices of baptism, churching of women, &c. much oftener ; whereas the primitive church never used it but once in one concourse of services. Free prayers has been objected to as liable to tautologies ; but surely the church can never urge this with the least propriety, many of the very same prayers occur both morning and evening. Indeed there is but little variation, except in the length. How often do they repeat, " Glory be to the Father, " and to the Son, and to the Holy Ghost ;" and in some churches this is done at the end of every psalm, besides the other places. In the Litany, " Good Lord " deliver us," is repeated eight times ; and " we beseech " thee to hear us good Lord," twenty-one times in half as many minutes. Prayers for the king are offered up thrice in the morning-service, with many other things of the like sort, which seem absolutely to contradict our Lord's precept, *When ye pray, use not vain repetitions*, Mat. vi. 7. The responses are at least too frequent, and with their continual risings up and sittings down, have oftentimes more of confused noise than appearance of devotion ; and may not the very frequent repetitions of the words, " O Lord, O God," bring many, especially of the younger sort, to that shocking habit of taking these holy names in vain. Notwithstanding the serious petition, " Lord have mercy " upon us, incline our hearts to keep this law ;" and it grieves me to observe, that the dissenters, whose honour it has heretofore been to be free from such looseness of expression, seem daily to be falling into it ; 'tis an awful truth, that the Lord will not hold such guiltless. The great Mr. Boyle never mentioned the venerable name of God, without making a pause, a noble example. The phrase, " our most religious king," in the prayer for the parliament, may in some reigns be highly improper ; and the term, " most gracious" is applied thrice times to Charles II. in the office for the twenty-ninth of May, though it is well known he had as little of grace as Nero had of Christianity ; the words being used in a civil sense will scarce

excuse

excuse it, in the service of God it is religiously applied.

Our usual custom of standing at prayer has been represented as very irreverent; but let those blush who say so, since Abra·ham stood before God, when he offered that humble supplication for Sodom, Gen. xviii. 22. Of the Levites and all the priests it is recorded, that they stood up; and all the people are called to stand up, and bless the Lord their God, in that solemn address, Neh. ix. 2, 3, 4, 5. Our Saviour represents two men praying in the temple standing, Luke xviii. 10, 11. yea himself in express words, has, if not actually enjoined, yet most fully declared his approbation of this gesture, Mark xi. 25. *When ye stand praying, forgive.* We should be more solicitous about the posture of the mind than the body; if that was so important, prostration, the most humble of all, ought to be used. In family worship, dissenters stand or kneel, as is most convenient, and any who chuse it may kneel in public. The shameful practice of staring about makes standing liable to objections.

The alternate repetition of the psalms by the minister and people is very improper. What sounds very well when spoken as the sentiment of David or Moses, when adopted as those of a Christian, and by this means it certainly has that appearance, loses all propriety, many things being applicable only to the Jews, and those who used the ceremonies of their law, which, in our days, many know little of, others are not suitable to the milder spirit of the gospel, especially the 109th. They are the wicked against whom these curses are denounced, and though excusable in a Jew, it becomes us to pray for the reformation, not the destruction of the worst, according to the dying example of our blessed Lord, Luke xxiii. 34. The 50th psalm, when read by any minister or other person, is excellent, but when thus read, by way of a dialogue, would lead one to think the parson and clerk were scolding.

Ver. 18, the parson says, " When thou sawest a " thief thou consentedst unto him : and hast been par- " taker with the adulterers."

The clerk answers, " Thou hast let thy mouth speak
· wickedness,

" wickednefs, and with thy tongue thou haft fet forth
" deceit."

Parfon rejoins, " Thou fatteft and fpakeft againft
" thy brother; yea, and haft flandered thy own mother's
" fon."

Clerk replies, " Thefe things has thou done, and I
" held my tongue ; and thou thoughteft wickedly, that
" I am even fuch a one as thyfelf ; but I will reprove
" thee, and fet before thee the things thou haft
" done."

This is not the only place where ferious matters are
thus burlefqu'd ; and not only the prayers, but even
the fcripture-leffons are appointed, and fo unequally
divided, that fome confift of lefs than ten, others of
fixty, and one of eighty verfes. It would be much
better if the minifter was permitted inftead of fome parts
of the Leviticus, and various genealogies, to chufe
the more plain and inftructive parts of fcripture, to
fay nothing of the fables (for the learned efteem them
no better) of Bel and the Dragon, Judith and Sufanna,
and above all, the ridiculous, improbable lie, in the 3d
of Tobit, about receiving the fair virgin from the
hands of her infernal lover, and conjuring away the
amorous devil Afmodæus, by the fumes of a fifhes liver.
To oblige minifters folemnly to read, if indeed they
can be read folemnly, fuch idle tales in the church, as
parts of public worfhip, is a monftrous impofition, a
difgrace to the fervice, and doing difhonour to Chriftianity thus to pollute its holy ordinances.

Befides ufing the liturgy, every minifter is obliged
alfo to declare, his unfeigned affent and confent to all
and every thing contained and prefcribed in and by the
book of common prayer.

Surely this is not acting as if the fcripture were the
only rule of faith ; and though all are obliged to make
this declaration, upon many it lies very heavy, confider-
able objections are to be made to the feveral offices, and
fome, which to an attentive reader will perhaps appear
unanfwerable. They fhall be mentioned in order, and
if there be found one thing in that book, one office or
form irrational, unfit, or repugnant to the gofpel fcheme,
furely whoever finds it fo, muft be hard put to it to
give

give an unlimited confent; for it is not to the general tenor, but to all and every thing in the book this muft be given.

The Athanafian creed, appointed to be read thirteen times every year, is, in our opinion, an abomination. Many eminent and good men in the church, have wifhed themfelves well rid of it, and fome there are who will not ufe it; but in this cafe they act contrary to thofe rules which their fubfcriptions oblige them to obey. Our pious fore fathers, though none could be more orthodox Trinitarians, fubfcribed the creed, but difliked the curfes, and protefted againft them, declaring that they did not confider the damnatory claufes as any part of the creed, nor give their affent to them. This was acting openly, and much better than the fhuffling pretence of a mental refervation, which fome who read it publicly in the folemn worfhip of God will pretend to. The creed itfelf is not fo intelligible and plain as to be edifying; there are few in comparifon who have any notion of what they are reading. How, then, can the unlearned fay Amen to it? But the curfes annexed are fhocking to a Chriftian ear, what can be faid to juftify them? Our Lord's faying, " he that believeth " not, fhall be damned," is alledged, but our Lord is fpeaking of his doctrines then delivered, and which were confirmed by fo many miracles; and this not merely for refufing affent to this doctrine, but on account of their bad hearts. *They would not come unto the light, left their deeds fhould be reproved,* John iii. 20. *and loved darknefs rather than light, becaufe their deeds were evil,* ver. 19. So, 2 Theff. ii. 12. fpeaking of thofe who fhould be damned that believed not the truth, adds, " but had pleafure in unrighteoufnefs." Moreover our Lord knew what was in man, and was therefore capable of paffing a judgment. How then can weak and fallible men pretend that this gives them a licence to denounce damnation againft fuch as do not affent to a creed of mere human invention, the language of which is to the greateft part of mankind, and even the learned, totally unintelligible. Had our reformers left this with the church of Rome, 'tis very probable many who now fubfcribe it, would have reprefented fuch arrogance as

the

the greateſt impiety, and becoming none but thoſe, whoſe mouths (againſt which as they call heretics) are full of curſing and bitterneſs. To ſay, it means to condemn the doctrines, not the perſons, concerning whom ſome hope may ſtill remain, is falſe; it is expreſly levelled againſt perſons, whoſoever does not keep whole and un-defiled therein delivered, he ſhall, without doubt, periſh everlaſtingly. Whoſoever, every one, which except a man believe, he. If notwithſtanding theſe deciſive and moſt peremptory declarations, this creed ſtill leaves any room to hope for the ſalvation of thoſe who oppoſe the faith therein delivered, the uſe of language is loſt, there is no meaning in words, and a man might ho-neſtly ſubſcribe the Koran of Mahomet, and reconcile it with the profeſſion of the goſpel of Chriſt. It muſt be difficult to many, in the preſence of God, the elect angels, and the church of Chriſt, to give their un-feigned aſſent and conſent to all and every thing con-tained in this creed, but whilſt not the ſmalleſt prefer-ment can be obtained in the church without this, many will ſwallow the bitter potion, and ſome even defend it ; and there are thoſe who will do the ſame by all the er-rors of popery. It is however well known, that many of the clergy deteſt and abhor theſe damnatory clauſes, and not a few who even ridicule the doctrines of it. What wonder then if religion declines, and a contempt of holy things ſo much prevails ? May it not almoſt be ſaid, that the reading this creed in the church thir-teen times every year, is more diſagreeable to God, (to whom alone vengeance belongeth) and more hurtful in its conſequences, than all the oaths ſworn in our navy and army within the ſame ſpace of time ?

As to the office of baptiſm there is this to object, that without the leaſt authority from reaſon and ſcrip-ture, or, as many ſay, from the antient practice of the church, the church of England has ſet aſide the parents in this ſolemnity, and forbid them to ſtand forth and take upon them the moſt important charge to which God and nature hath called them; for the 29th canon expreſly commands, " That no parent ſhall be " urged to be preſent at his child's baptiſm, nor be " admitted to anſwer as godfather for his own child."

Other

Other persons are required to appear in the parents stead, and take upon them this important trust. It is not pretended that there is any foundation for this practice in scripture, the reason alledged is, that there may be a double security for the child's education; but as it is pretty certain that such persons scarce ever think of fulfilling this trust, so to make this appear plausible, persons of good character ought to be appointed ; and it is ordered by the 29th canon just cited, that none shall stand who have not received the sacrament. In country churches, I am certain, this is little attended to, besides it is further necessary, if this be the reason, that godfathers and godmothers should be of suitable age ; whereas very old persons are often chosen for this purpose, concerning whom there is not the least probability they should ever live to see this done ; and if the parents are likewise advanced, such can never answer the end. Parents are certainly more interested in this affair than any, they ought therefore at least to be suffered to answer for their children, who would chuse it, and those who prefer the other method, retain their liberty.

The vows made are very solemn. This infant, says the office, must promise by you that are his sureties, until he comes of age to take it upon himself, that he will renounce the devil, and all his works, and continually believe God's holy words, and obediently keep his commandments ; and they are in the name of the child to renounce the devil, and all his works, &c. these are promises which there is no possibility of performing, and to say it means as far as lies in their power, is indeed softening the matter; but the promise is absolute, and no room left for such a latitude. The celebrated champions for the church differ in explaining this mysterious affair. Mr. White says, the church considers these as the child's answers, only by its representatives ; they contain its part of the baptismal covenant, which, because of its tender age itself cannot utter, is uttered by its sureties. This is to the highest degree ridiculous, for the child has no thought, no understanding, no conception of these things ; it cannot be considered or supposed, as being any otherwise than merely passive

passive in the affair, Dr. Nichols a much greater man, differs much herein, for he says, the sureties religiously engaged for the truth of the baptized, that they should sincerely believe all that was revealed in the gospel, and direct the subsequent actions of their lives by the law of Christ. Surely it is somewhat rash to promise so much for another, and is certainly more than any person can engage to do. If this institution is so useful (and even necessary as some have termed it, and indeed if it is not why, should it be imposed?) since it is now become a mere matter of form, and the negligence of sponsors so general as to defeat any good designs intended by it, the church ought to exert itself in correcting these abuses. The ceremony of signing with the cross has been already considered.

Many have thought that the answer to this question in the catechism, What is required of persons to be baptized? is entirely inconsistent with the practice of infant baptism. The answer is, Repentance, whereby they forsake sin, and faith, whereby they stedfastly believe the promises of God made to them in that sacrament. They cannot repent, because they have no sin to forsake ; if original sin be meant it is weak, for the child knows nothing about it, and as to having faith in the promises of God, it is impossible, for faith as St. Paul says, comes by hearing them, Rom. x. 17. but how can they believe of what they have not heard? The following question and answer do not seem to mend the matter. Q. Why then are infants baptized when by reason of their tender age they cannot perform them? An. Because they promise them both by their sureties, which promise when they come to age, themselves are bound to perform. But the children promise neither, and if the sureties did it for them, it was entirely without their consent, desire or knowledge, and so the promise lays them under no obligation. Which promise themselves when they come to age are bound to perform, is allowed, and so they would if no such promise had been made, or if they had not been baptized at all. Dissenters who consider infant baptism as a rite appointed by God, look on it as a standing token of his mercy and grace to them, a perpetual memorial instituted

tuted in the church signifying to believers, God's readiness to pour down his spirit and blessing upon them and their infant offspring, and the parents (or if they die, the obligation comes upon some other person) enter into a solemn engagement to bring up their children in the nurture and admonition of the Lord, the child neither promises nor is supposed to promise any thing, but is merely passive.

The next office is that of confirmation. The only text of scripture urged for it is Acts viii. 14. Dr. Whitby and perhaps most of the clergy who do not catch at sound, instead of sense, acknowledge it to be nothing to the purpose. Peter and John being sent by the apostles to lay their hands on those whom Philip had baptized and converted, is no precedent for our bishops to do the same. The design was that they might receive the holy ghost, that is the miraculous gifts, such as prophesying and speaking with tongues, visible and obvious to the senses, for when Simon saw, &c. see v. 18. But our bishops are too wise and modest to pretend to such powers, and as to what are by them called the ordinary gifts of the holy ghost, we considered when speaking of the office of consecration, and shewed that one could no more be conveyed than the other. Neither will this passage make any thing for confirmation, unless the apostles laid their hands on all who were baptized, and if they were then Simon must be confirmed and receive the holy ghost; but this was not the case, and since it was necessary that the apostles themselves should come down to confer on them these gifts, the power must cease with them.

The business of confirmation is as follows, by order of the liturgy, all persons baptized when they come to competent years, and are able to say the Lord's prayer, creed, and ten commandments, and the answers of the shorter catechism are to be brought to confirmation. The bishop having asked them, whether they renew the solemn promise and vow which was made in their names in baptism; upon their answering we do, proceeds hereupon to declare in a most solemn manner, even in an address to God himself, that he (God) has vouchsafed to regenerate these his servants by water and the
holy

holy Ghoft, and to give them the forgivenefs of all their fins, and laying his hand upon the head of each particular perfon, he certifies him by that fign, of God's favour and gracious goodnefs to him. I defy the moft learned man upon earth to tell me, what warrant any bifhop has to pronounce a man's fins all forgiven and himfelf regenerated by the holy Ghoft, upon no better grounds than his being able to fay the fhorter catechifm, and declaring that he ftands by his baptifmal covenant. This is not the fcripture doctrine of acceptance with God; nor are the moft folemn vows and promifes any proof of regeneration, for it is not every one that fayeth Lord, Lord, fhall enter into the kingdom of heaven, and a man's barely profefling to repent, and promifing to live godly, is not that actual repentance and amendment of life, which can alone fecure the divine pardon and favour. How can any man dare prefume upon fuch grounds, to affure a perfon that he is regenerated and in a ftate of favour with God? This however the bifhop does, and to fatisfy every doubt as far as poffible, lays his hand upon his head to certify him by that fign of God's favour and goodnefs to him. This practice has a very dangerous tendency; many upon fuch a declaration from this facred perfon, whom they are taught to look upon as an ambaffador of Chrift, a fucceffor of the apoftles and a fpecial minifter of God, are almoft led to believe that they have full remiffion of their fins, and that their fouls are in a fafe ftate; and as thefe are to be obtained on fuch eafy terms, it is no wonder fo many hundreds flock to receive fo vaft a benefit; the manner of fpending the day at thefe feafons, affords but little proof of any good change being worked in them or good difpofitions inftilled. Thus they fay peace, peace, where there is no peace, or look upon the whole as a folemn farce, and the naturally be led to defpife all the ordinances of religion. Such are the fad confequences of departing from the fimplicity of the gofpel by introducing human ordinances. Chrift and his apoftles never as we have heard of, appointed any rite after baptifm but the Lord's fupper. Every difciple of Chrift is in duty bound to make this profeffion of faith in an obedience to him, let us

D   chufe

obferve this inftitution, and not being confirmed will never be any lofs to us.

As to the ceremonies to be ufed in marriage, there is nothing faid in fcripture, and here therefore we may lawfully fubmit to the eftablifhed forms and to fuch ceremonies as the civil magiftrate appoints. Its being done in a church does not make it any otherwife than a civil act, becaufe one building is as holy as another, fince there can be no religion in ftones or wood, in whatever form put together, and the prayers, paftoral charge, &c. do not alter the cafe, fince an oath taken in a common court of judicature has the fame appendages and every whit as folemn, you fhall fwear to the truth, &c. is a charge, and fo help me God, a prayer, as truly as thofe offered in a church. The puritans fcrupled the ufe of the ring as being a popifh cuftom, and it might have been as well dropt, though there is no harm in ufing it, nor would there in a bracelet or necklace, if the law appointed either of thefe in its ftead, or added them to it. The words, with my body I thee worfhip, have been fcrupled by fome, but lovers are ufually complaifant, and therefore the expreffion may be excufed, fince all are fuppofed to be fuch, at leaft before the knot is tied, it may alfo be confidered as an equivalent to the honour and obey, which difpleafes fo many fair ones. The refufing to marry in Lent, in the fame manner as at other feafons in the year, may perhaps be that nothing may interrupt fo folemn a faft; however, it feems to refemble no very good character which the apoftle fpeaks of, 1 Tim. iv. 3. one part of which was, forbidding to marry.

Now I grow ferious again. The abfolution in the office for vifiting the fick, we ftrongly object to, as it favours too much of rank popery. Let the fick perfon have been ever fo vile and profligate, the prieft is directed after fome previous exhortations to examine whether he believes the articles of the apoftles creed, and truly repents him of his fin, and be in charity with all the world, and to move him to make a fpecial confeffion of his fins, if he feels his confcience troubled with any weighty matter. After which if he humbly and heartily defire it, the prieft is to abfolve him in the following words.

words. " Our Lord Jesus Christ, who hath left all power
" to his church to absolve all sinners who truly repent
" and believe in him, of his great mercy forgive thee
" thine offences; and by his authority committed to me,
" I absolve thee from all these sins, in the name of the
" Father, and of the Son, and of the holy Ghost. Amen."

How solemn this form! how weighty this matter! but
without good grounds, such a proceeding is trifling
with the great name of God, and invading the authority of the supreme judge. The apostles had authority to declare, repent and be converted that your
sins may be blotted out, Acts iii. 19. and God hath
promised to forgive all such as truly repent, but the
presumptuous language I absolve thee, is not to be
found in scripture, nor because God hath promised to
forgive all who repent, can any power be derived to
declare this forgiveness to any particular person, merely
on account of their professions, for not every one that
saith unto me Lord, Lord, &c. Mat. vii. 21. and surely
those of men on a sick and dying bed, cannot be depended upon as signs of true penitence. In the near
prospect of eternity, they begin to be alarmed and to cry
out for help, but these arising merely from terror are
seldom lasting, of which we see sad evidences in most
wicked men who recover, for they again turn to folly.
Their humbly and heartily desiring it is no reason why
it should be given, for the vilest wretch on earth
would desire and that with strong crying and tears, to
have his sins remitted, if such fervent desire would pre-
serve him from the consequences of them. And to
what purpose is it to exhort to present repentance, solemnly to warn men not to trust to the sorrows of a sick
bed, if there are a number of men obliged, (and the clergy
are obliged and dare not refuse if required) in the name
of the Father, Son and holy Ghost to absolve him from
all his sins, how great and heinous soever, and thus declare him fully forgiven? Christ gave to his apostles
power to remit and to retain sins, but what does this
mean? not that persons should be by them absolved,
upon their bare professions, and that after a whole life
spent in wickedness, but that they should preach the
gospel and declare that those who submitted to the terms

of

of it fhould have their fins remitted, Luke xxiv. 47. Acts ii. 38.—xiii. 38, 39. and confequently thofe who would not that their fins fhould be retained and render them liable to condemnation. This is very different from what the church lays claim to; and furely if the apoftles never abfolved a man from his fins, only declared they would be forgiven on their repentance, though they had the holy fpirit and fuch a knowledge of the heart, fee Acts v. as none can now pretend to; what a monftrous impiety for fallible men, and efpecially bad men, for I know and fpeak it with forrow that fometimes a minifter is as vile and wicked as the worft in the parifh, to affume fo great a power, fo facred a truft. It fills me with horror, to hear men declare in the name of God, they have fuch a power as they can produce no commiffion for, and to make ufe of it in deceiving men in an affair of infinite importance, the falvation of their immortal fouls, which the fcripture tells us muft be fecured by a patient continuance in well doing.

Adminiftring the facrament to the fick, never appears to have been the defign of the ordinance. It is a ftanding memorial of the death of Chrift, and always publicly kept by the apoftles and their followers. If the fick perfon has been a good man, and remembered the Lord's death at his table in the affemblies of his faints, he has done all that is required; if he has neglected this, doing it now would not anfwer the end of making a public profeffion of his faith in Chrift, a fincere refolution to do this if health returns, a good God will accept of; but if the perfon has been a finner, (and to the greateft, fuch as are going to be cut off by the hands of juftice for the moft flagrant crimes, it is adminiftered) it may tend to fill him with falfe hopes, whilft at the fame time it will be no more fervice to his foul, than phyfic to a dead carcafe.

The burial fervice is drawn up with an awful folemnity, but there are paffages in it entirely inexcufable, incapable of a fober vindication. Dr. Bennet, (a true fon of the church) acknowledges as much, fince he fays, " It was never intended to be ufed at the burial of fuch " perfons, as die in a ftate of notorious impenitence,
without

" withort any appearance or profeffion of their return"
" to God. I hope therefore that none of my brethren,
" will ever proftitute this facred fervice, to the worft of
" purpofes, to the encouragement of vice and the har-
" dening of finners; and that they will never change
" the whole of it into one continued and deliberate
" falfehood by fo fcandalous a mifapplication." So fays
that learned and high church doctor. But is not this
office ufed indifcriminately? Can any clergyman refufe to read it over the moft fcandalous and hardened
finner? he cannot without acting contrary to the
rubric, and expofing himfelf to a fevere profecution.
There are but three cafes in which it can be refufed:
To fuch as die unbaptized, to felf-murderers, and to
thofe who are under the greater excommunication.
But if men have lived in all excefs of riot, if a mur-
derer in attempting the life of an innocent perfon fhould
be himfelf flain, or a criminal cut off by the hands of
juftice for fome atrocious crime, dying hardened and
impenitent, concerning whom, God hath fworn that
they fhall not enter into his reft; yet, aftonifhing to relate, contrary to the reafon of mankind, contrary to
what the moft extenfive charity would lead us to
conclude, contrary to what the fcripture repeatedly
affirms; the church of England neverthelefs commands its minifters moft folemnly to declare over
fuch, That almighty G..d has of his great mercy,
taken to himfelf the foul of this our dear brother, here
departed, and that when they know he was taken
away in his wrath; they give God hearty thanks that
it hath pleafed him to deliver him out of the miferies
of this finful world, when there is the ftrongeft reafon
to believe that he is gone to greater miferies below,
and pray God that when they fhall depart out of life,
they may reft in him, as their hope is this their brother
doth. But what ground is there for hope, fince where
Chrift is, nothing that is defiled fhall enter? This fervice gives the lie to all thofe ferious exhortations which
faithful minifters are continually giving to a devout
and holy life, and contradicts all the arguments they
draw from fcripture, concerning the future mifery of
thofe who live after the flefh. To declare in the pulpit
that without holinefs no man fhall fee the Lord; and

within

within an hour perhaps declare, at the grave of one of the vileſt and wicked in the pariſh, a ſure and certain hope of his reſurrection to eternal life, (that is happineſs, as the word always ſignifies in ſcripture, and in this place, or it will not be an object of hope.) Expreſſions ſufficiently high and confident, even at the funeral of an apoſtle, muſt give encouragement to vice, or expoſe the ſervice to the contempt of men of the leaſt reflection.

And what is moſt ſtrange and aſtoniſhing of all, is the more than a miracle which the church performs, in damning and ſaving the ſame individual perſons. Arians and Socinians, the church declares in its famous creed, will, without doubt, periſh everlaſtingly. Yet no ſooner are they dead, though they died firmly eſtabliſhed in the doctrines which Athanaſius damned, the church ſolemnly declares that God hath, in great mercy, taken them to himſelf, and that it hopes they reſt in Chriſt. But what room is there to hope for thoſe, who, without doubt, periſh everlaſtingly? Surely none. "To "ſay that the hereſies are damnable, and the perſons who "eſpouſe them liable to damnation ; yet that there may "be room for pardon in particular caſes, and when one "of them dies it may be charitably hoped, that his is "ſuch a caſe that we do not quite deſpair is trifling." The Athanaſian creed expreſly damns the perſons, and every perſon, to talk of pardon and hope, in particular caſes, is nothing to the purpoſe ; the ſervice is read over all that die, no one caſe is excepted but the three abovementioned. The language uſed is not that of not quite deſpairing, 'tis the moſt confident words will admit. They thank God that he hath in great mercy taken the departed ſoul to himſelf, and pray they may reſt in Chriſt, as their hope is this Arian or Socinian doth, who, without doubt, ſays the creed, ſhall periſh everlaſtingly. Conſidering theſe in connection, and a churchman muſt, or acknowledge he agrees to inconſiſtencies ; what is it but — the expreſſion is ſhocking, but really it is nothing leſs than to pray, that they may be damned ? This being the caſe with Arians and Socinians, how much greater the inconſiſtency when a Deiſt is buried, who ſo far from acknowledging Chriſt

to

to have had any connection with the Deity, look upon him as a bold impoftor. Till the Athanafian creed is rejected, or the burial-fervice altered, the church acts moft ftrangely, for out of the fame mouth proceeds bleffing and curfing, which, St. James tells us, ought not to be. I appeal to every Chriftian, whether a fo-lemn affent and confent to all and every thing con-tained in the book of common prayer, may not well be fcrupled, and whether we have not reafon to ufe other forms, and other methods ?

The church of England maintains a threefold order of minifters. Deacons, who may perform any office, except adminiftering the facrament, (at which they can only affift) and pronouncing the abfolution. Priefts, who may perform all the offices, and bifhops, to whom alone belongs the power of confirming baptifed per-fons, ordaining minifters, confecrating churches and church-yards, and, as they would have men believe, of governing the church ; though, in this refpect, their hands are fo tied down by the civil power, that they have nothing but the name ; for all the bifhops united cannot alter a tittle in the church-fervice, or make the moft trifling alteration in any thing that belongs to it. The law indeed has given them liberty to refufe confer-ring orders on fuch as they fhall deem unfit, but if a clergyman is prefented to a living, however unfit or unqualified he may be, they cannot deny him inftitution into it, without expofing themfelves to a law-fuit, which they may probably lofe, and this is a rifk they do not chufe to run.

Deacons are not properly an order of minifters, being firft appointed to take care of the poor, fee Acts vi. who were overfeers. That fome of them preached is certain, as Stephen and Philip, but not the more on account of their being of that order, but becaufe they had the gift of the holy Ghoft.

Prieft is a name never applied to minifters of the gofpel in the New Teftament ; the name perhaps is retained to fupport their pretended divine right to tithes, which were with great reafon paid to the Jewifh priefts, fince they were, as being of the tribe of Levi, excluded from any fhare in the divifion of the
land ;

land; but this not being the cafe with the former, and not meeting a word to favour this claim, as defcending to them, they took the name for a covering.

But prefbyters or elders, (or priefts, as the church commonly calls them) and bifhops, are not diftinct orders, but different names for the fame perfons. The church at Philippi had but two orders of church-officers amongft them, bifhops and deacons, Phil. i. 1. The name, office, and work of a bifhop and prefbyter are the fame. " For this caufe left I thee in Crete, that " thou fhouldeft ordain elders," that is, prefbyters (which is the meaning of the word elder, in our lan- guage, and the fame word in the original, though our tranflation has adopted two of the fame import) " in " every city, for a bifhop muft be blamelefs." Tit. i. 5, 7. Paul called the prefbyters of the church of Ephe- fus together, and charged them to take heed to the flock, over which the holy Ghoft had made them bi- fhops. Our tranflations have it, * overfeers, which is not improper, fince it is the duty of a bifhop to infpect into the conduct of his flock, Acts xx. 27, 28. fo 1. Pet. v. 1, 2. " The prefbyters among you I exhort, " who alfo am a prefbyter, feed the flock of God among " you, taking the overfight thereof;" that is, perform- ing the office of bifhops, as the word επισκοπευντες im- ports. And indeed the fuperiority of bifhops to pref- byters, has been acknowledged by the firft reformers, and founders of the church of England, and many of its learned doctors fince, not to be of divine, but only of human inftitution, not founded upon fcripture, but only upon the cuftom or ordinances of this realm.

What right then our diocefan bifhops have to ufurp the bufinefs of ordination, as belong only to them, ex- cluding all others from that office, is hard to guefs. And yet we are often told that we have neither minif- ters, facraments, nor ordinances, and that our minifters can never expect a bleffing upon their labours, nor the people any benefit from them, for want of their epifco- pal ordination. Sad, indeed, was this really the cafe, fince the churches in Scotland, and thofe of the pro-

---

* It is probable this was artfully done by the tranflators, leaft the name elders and bifhops being fo plainly applied to the fame perfons, might have embarraffed them in their difputes with the puritans.

teftants

teſtants abroad, both in Europe, and great part of America, have no other than preſbyterian ordination. In Denmark there are what they call biſhops, but as the firſt proteſtant prelates received ordination from Bugenhagius, a mere preſbyter, they can have conveyed nothing more to their ſucceſſors. And whence do the church of England biſhops derive this power? they muſt acknowledge that all their validity is derived from the idolatrous church of Rome; yes, this is neceſſary to keep up their pretended, uninterrupted ſucceſſion, and apoſtolic deſcent. But they abuſe this their good mother, from whom they derive theſe mighty powers, in a ſtrange manner, in one of the homilies; to which every clergyman ſubſcribes, as containing a good and wholeſome doctrine. This homily ſays, " that the church of " Rome is idolatrous, and anti-chriſtian, not only a har- " lot, as the ſcripture calleth her, but alſo a foul, filthy, " withered, old harlot, the fouleſt and filthieſt that ever " was ſeen, and that it at preſent is and hath been for " nine hundred years, it is far from the nature of a " true church, that nothing can be more."—What miracles are here! That which is no true church, nor has been any thing like for eleven hundred years paſt (it is now more than two hundred years ſince the homilies were compoſed, and Rome is not altered ſince) yet conveys true, regular, church-offices and powers, and an anti-apoſtolic church imparts genuine apoſtolic orders. Can a filthy and corrupt harlot produce any other than a corrupt breed? She may bring forth children it may be ſaid better than herſelf, but the children muſt be born in a ſtate of fornication, a ſpurious race. However if a prieſt ordained, with all the ſuperſtitious and idolatrous rites of this antichriſtian and falſe church, comes over to the church of England, he is admitted as a brother duly ordained; but if a miniſter of any of the reformed churches joins himſelf to them, he is conſidered only as a layman, an unordained perſon, and is obliged to receive ordination again, according to their forms. No, the hand and devout prayers of the moſt learned, virtuous, religious, and chriſtian preſbyters of Scotland, Geneva, or any ſuch proteſtant churches, are not ſo efficacious, it ſeems, to

send

fend forth a true minifter of the church of Chrift, as
the hands and fuperftitious prayers of an anti-chriftian,
idolatrous, perfecuting, and wicked bifhop of Spain
or Italy. The prelates of the proteftant church build
their power of ordaining minifters, and adminiftering
divine ordinances, upon the orders received from this
mother of harlots; if fuch a fountain, however, imparts any thing, it can be but impure and foul. I
appeal to common fenfe, whether a man is not as well
qualified for the miniftry, who is fet apart to it, by
proteftant divines, who are, in reality, as much bifhops, according to the fcripture fenfe, though not the
common application of the word, as my lord of
Canterbury or London.

Befides, we do not fee a proper agreement between
the bifhops of the church of England, and the apoftolic ones. The very word bifhop is derived from
ἐπισκοπεῖν, which fignifies to overlook or infpect, but
it is impoffible ours can do it. Bifhoprics here take
in a county, or two, or more. Lincoln includes, not
only that large county, but likewife all Leicefterfhire,
Huntingdon, Bedford, Bucks, and part of Hertford.
The large and populous cities of London and Weft-
minfter, the counties of Middlefex, Effex, part of
Hertfordfhire, with all the churches in the eaft and
weft Indies, are under the bifhop of London's care;
who is fufficient for thefe things? Read the epiftles, to
the bifhops, of Timothy and Titus, and fee wherein
they are to refemble our lord bifhops. So far are the
latter from being apt to teach, that the Welch ones
do not underftand the language of the people over
whom they are fet: They are more in the palace than
in the pulpit, and oftentimes more at court than in
their diocefes. Neither do they encourage teaching
in others, fince they frequently beftow livings on their
favourites, who have one or two before; the neceffary
confequence of which is, that fome of the parifhes muft
be left to curates, with perhaps a fifth, and often
much lefs, of the income. The beft excufe which
can be made for them is, that they are only civil officers; and this is the truth of the cafe. Pray, in
what part of the fcripture do we read of lord bifhops?

nor

nor have the clergy any thing to do in the choice of them, but juſt ſo far as to render the affair ridiculous, if not impious. The king ſends the dean and chapter a commiſſion to elect a new biſhop, and a letter, recommending (as it is called, for they dare not at the peril of looſing their preferment, chuſe any other) ſome particular divine. On receiving this, the dean and chapter meet to pray God in a moſt ſolemn manner, that he would direct them in their choice ; (when it is but Hobſon's choice ; and perhaps the perſon has been mentioned in the public papers long before their commiſſion arrives) they always fix upon the perſon named, whoever he is, and yet, in another prayer, return thanks to God for directing them to the choice of ſo worthy a perſon, though they know that they were wholly directed by the court, and that, as it ſometimes happens, to a very unworthy man. And, is it not a little droll, that when the biſhop is to be conſecrated, though he and his friends have been uſing all their intereſt for years to procure him that office, ſhould nevertheleſs three times ſay, *nolo epiſcopaci*, I am unwilling to be a biſhop. All this is really ſhocking to ſober Chriſtians, and extremely diverting no doubt to deiſts, who will make a handle of ſuch things to ridicule the whole. As for arch-biſhops, deans, arch deacons, canons, prebendaries, &c. on whom ſuch immenſe revenues are beſtowed, it is ſufficient to ſay, that there is not the leaſt mention of them in any part of ſcripture ; and that they are derived from the ſame ſource with popes, cardinals, abbots, monks, friars, and all the uſeleſs herds of prieſts with which popiſh countries ſwarm.

Some indeed have ſaid, that deans, prebendaries, &c. are uſeful in attending prayers in the cathedral ; but are thoſe prayers ſo very acceptable to God which they have, perhaps, hundreds per annum for offering ? and what becomes of this mighty benefit, when the ſame perſon who has a prebend in the north, has a biſhopric in the ſouth, and a cure of ſouls in the heart of the kingdom. Similar things frequently happen, and there are ſuch caſes even now, to ſay nothing of the time ſpent in court attendance, levee

hunting,

hunting, &c. As for the hospitality of these dignitaries, few cathedral towns know any thing of it.

That every lay-christian has a right to chose his own pastor, is so plain from scripture, reason, and the practice of the primitive church, that as the very learned Mr. William Lowth, a zealous churchman acknowledges, it can be only ignorance or folly that will plead the contrary. Any one would naturally conclude, that as every man has a natural right to chuse his own physician or lawyer, and that it would be very hard to have one forced upon him, whose abilities he distrusted, so if the welfare of the soul be equal to that of the body, and every good christian thinks it superior, it is undoubtedly both fit and necessary that every one should chuse his minister to instruct him in holy things. This is very clear from scripture; the charges given to Christians to take heed what they hear, to beware of false prophets, not to believe every spirit, but to try the spirits, evidently suppose a power to judge of the qualifications of ministers, and to reject such as they disapproved. When an apostle was to be chosen in the room of Judas the traytor, the whole body of the disciples appointed, by their common suffrage, two candidates for that office. The election was indeed referred to God, but if the choice of one of the two was the act of God, that of two from the whole number, was the act of the whole society; and it is very probable, if they had been unanimous, they would not have referred it to God at all, since the almighty was not displeased with not being first consulted, see Acts i. When the apostles wanted persons to assist them, they did not fix upon them, though undoubtedly well qualified for it, but said, 'Wherefore, brethren, look out from amongst yourselves, seven men of honest report, and the multitude chose Stephen, &c.' Acts vi. If it should be asked, supposing the majority of a congregation should chose one whom many dislike, what must be done? We say, no one is obliged to submit to the majority, every person is to chuse for himself, whoever does not approve the minister chosen, is at liberty to withdraw from the society. Churches ought always

to proceed in choofing a minifter with great feriouf-
nefs and deliberation; and the principal fupporters
of a congregation, or even the majority of it, do
wrong to bring in a minifter difagreeable to many of
the people, and indeed 'tis not every minifter will
accept fuch a call. It has likewife been objected,
that the minifter may furvive the greateft part, or even
all who choofe him, and the fociety be entirely compofed of perfons who were born, or came to it after
his election; but furely, if perfons join voluntarily
to a fociety, it is a fign they approve the minifter,
and then it is of no confequence if they were not at his
firft choice, fince they as much choofe him as if they
were. It is very unlikely, though it be poffible, that
he fhould outlive the greateft number; but if it fhould
fo happen, a worthy character will recommend himfelf
to the young, who have been always under his care, and
if they difapprove him, they have a liberty to attend
any other. A minifter is always chofen by thofe who
join his church, as much as if they were prefent at the
firft choice. Make the moft of thefe objections, many
remain pleafed, and generally a very large majority;
but it often happens in the church, that very few, or
none, approve the perfon forced on them, and very large
congregations have expreffed the ftrongeft diflike to their
minifters, without being able to obtain redrefs. I wonder that our brethren of the eftablifhment can fubmit to
fuch ufage, and that they do not, on fuch occafions, choofe
and fupport a minifter they do approve of to adminifter
to them according to the eftablifhed forms, rather than
bear fuch an impofition; 'tis true, even then they may
be refufed the ufe of the parifh church, though perhaps,
the rector might confent to it, otherwife, they muft
put up with the inconvenience, or affemble within un-
confecrated walls, without tower or bells, which would
perhaps look too much like a meeting. What renders
this ftill the more irkfome is, that in parifhes where the
tythes amount to feveral fcores, or even hundreds, per
annum, inftead of being ferved by the rector or vicar,
the care of the parifh is left to a poor curate, whom
they hire as cheap as they can, whofe pittance is fo
fmall, that he can fcarce fupport his family with decency,

cency, much lefs fhew any good example, by charity
to the poor. Sometimes two, three, or even four parifhes are fupplied by the fame perfon, (in what manner any one may guefs) whilft he who has all the profits,
fits, feldom or never comes to the place. I know of
a very large town in the weft, where the vicar has not
been for many years, but holds two livings befides, at
a great diftance, and is chiefly employed in rural di-
verfions; 'tis to be feared there are many fuch inftan-
ces. With what propriety then can the church of
England be called, the beft conftituted church in the
world ?

The bifhops may rectify this matter if they will,
fince there are laws obliging the clergy to refidence.
But here is the evil? It often happens, and is the cafe
with fome of the prefent bifhops, that, befides a bifhopric in the north or eaft, they are rectors of fome
parifh in the fouth or weft, and then, as they cannot
refide upon both (though by a ftatute of the 21ft of
Henry VIII. a bifhop is punifhable if he be not refident upon his parfonage, neither will his being conftantly on his diocefe excufe him) as the evil would fall
upon themfelves, they fhamefully wink at the matter;
and even arch-deacons, who are termed one of the eyes
of the bifhop, are fo far from always refiding, (though
the law fays, if they are abfent for one month together, or two months in the year, they fhall pay 10 l.
for each fault) that even bifhops themfelves hold arch-
deaconries, and that in their own diocefes. The bifhop of Bangor, is alfo arch-deacon of Bangor and
Anglefea; the bifhop of St. Afaph, arch-deacon of St.
Afaph, though the only one belonging to that fee.
What a ftrange accumulation of preferments, utterly
inconfiftent with each other, and of the moft fatal
tendency to the difcipline and good order of the diocefe, as well as an ill example to the clergy !

I could greatly enlarge here, but thefe abfurdities
muft ftrike every man who will but reflect a moment.
Indeed, when I reflect on the large revenues many
of the clergy have who do nothing, the fmall pittances
of thofe who bear all the burden, the number of worth-
lefs men who have two or three livings, and the many
learned

learned and worthy ones who have but pitiful curacies, together with the shameful manner in which some parishes are served, where there is a decent, and even affluent income for the ministers, and all this in a country where the tenths of so many articles, besides lands and other perquisites are bestowed on the clergy; yet after all, that the people should be deprived of their just and undoubted right of choosing their own ministers; I can scarce write or think without indignation. This is the true cause of the clergy's being so backward in having the most glaring errors altered, (it was thus at the reformation from popery, that glorious work was opposed by the clergy, particularly by those in the highest stations.) They do not know where a reformation once begun would end, it cannot be through a regard for the articles, their writings contradict them, but they regard their preferments, which they well know, neither the laws of God or of reason will suffer them to hold. Bishops may send pastoral letters, and deliver solemn charges, the clergy may write books in defence of Christianity, and defend it from the pulpit with all the powers of eloquence; but as long as their practice is so inconsistent with the rules of the gospel, no person can believe their zeal is for Christianity, but for the church, (its revenues) it cannot be for Christ, 'tis for the craft. A noble lord, the most noble in the British senate, if virtue and learning can make him so, being asked the reason why so many of our great men ran into deism? replied, "It was owing to the conduct of the bishops, for seeing those act so inconsistent with the rules of the gospel, who, they supposed must understand its evidences, inclined them to think it was all a farce." How long the laity will suffer this spiritual wickedness in high places, I know not; this seems to be a thinking age; and when men apply themselves a little to think of religion, there may be a reformation. Till there is, Christianity can never be supported on the present footing of the establishment; therefore, it is of the highest importance to it, that the dissenting interest should be supported. The dissenting interest, I say, that has been the bulwark against tyranny, against po-

pery,

pery, and againſt deiſm. The writings in defence of
our holy religion by Chandler, Doddridge, Foſter,
Leland, Lardner, and other ſuch men, who, ſooner
than make ſhipwreck of a good conſcience, or betray
its intereſt for gain, depended entirely on the benevo-
lence of their people, though they might have been made
independant, and raiſed, without doubt, to the high-
eſt dignities in the church, perferment being actually
refuſed by ſome of them, will be read with attention and
patience: But when men, who have ſworn to articles
which their preaching often contradicts, when they
claim powers, which the goſpel they defend declares
does not belong to them; when they recommend the
conduct of a humble Jeſus, and his poor apoſtles, and
yet accumulate revenues, claim lordly titles, and buſy
themſelves ſo much in civil affairs, while the intereſt
of religion is declining, where they may, where they
ought, where they ſolemnly promiſe to be preſent to
ſupport it; when ſuch men publiſh defences of Chriſtianity, what ſucceſs can they expect? Religion is
wounded through their ſides: But diſſenters chuſe their
own paſtors, and have therefore no non-reſidents, no
pluraliſts, (for the few miniſters in and about London,
who have two congregations divided betwixt two, cannot be ſo called) and their miniſters are full as re-
ſpectable a body as the eſtabliſhed ciergy, and, conſidering their numbers, have produced as many ingenious, learned, and I am ſure, uſeful men. They
have even made the clergy better; many of them have
complained, that in towns where the preſbyterians have
meetings, they have been obliged to preach twice a
day leaſt the people ſhould leave the church; thus have
they been kept to their duty againſt their will. I never knew a town leſs virtuous, leſs ſober, and leſs regular for having diſſenters in it; but I have known,
that where the intereſt has declined, they have dege-
nerated from this character, with regard to obſerving
the Lord's day particularly.

I hope, from this ſhort view, it will plainly appear,
that the principles of our diſſent, ſo far from being
trifling, as is ſo often inſinuated in various books,
and on various occaſions, are of the utmoſt importance

tance to religion ; and likewife, that fuch as are convinced of it, fo far from being afhamed of their d.f-
fent, will glory in it, and ftand up for pure, genuine,
fcripture Chriftianity, in oppofition to any new editions
with corrections and amendments, with additional
fplendors, and new terms of communion, befides thofe
which Chrift made. The church of Rome has done
this ; and, to every impartial enquirer it will appear,
that another church has followed her example. You
will perhaps be called fchifmatics, and fchifm is a
word about which ecclefiaftics have made a fearful
noife ; often, very often, we fchifmatics have been
damned to the pit of hell, and by the more moderate,
treated as obftinate and factious perfons. But this
faid word, my friends, is nothing more than an ecclefiaftical fcarecrow, fit to terrify the weak, but very
contemptible to men of fenfe. Priefts of all countries
and all religions, will ring changes on this their favourite word, and fchifm, fchifm ; fchifmatics, fchifmatics ; will always be the cry againft thofe who fhall
oppofe their fuperftitions. The church of Rome lays
this charge on the church of England full as liberally
as fhe can on the diffenters ; and how does fhe defend
herfelf? not by her 20th article nor by the 34, no ;
when a jefuit attacks her, armed cap a-pee, then fathers, authority, church power, the danger of fchifm,
about which her friends talk fo gravely to us, are all
flung away. Then the bible, the bible only is the religion of proteftants ; every man is to read and judge
for himfelf, then not thofe who feparate from a church,
which impofes unfcriptural terms, is guilty of fchifm,
but the church alone which impofes fuch terms. This
is good proteftant reafoning ; we ftick to it, and therefore, feparate from a church, which impofes unfcriptural terms of communion, which claims authority in
controverfies of faith, and have as much reafon to
call the church of England fchifmatical, as fhe has that
of Rome. We can do this with a better grace, becaufe we allow to no church fuch authority, but they
do, and it will be very hard to prove, that their church
has a better right to do this than that of Rome or Ruffia. The primitive Chriftians were looked upon as

E 3   fchifmatics

schismatics by the heathen priests; and should any one
of our bishops, out of his great zeal for Christianity, tra-
vel into Turkey or China to make converts, the Muf-
ties and Bonzees would soon stir up the populace by
the same cry. The apostle Paul speaks of divisions or
schisms, and prayed they might cease : what these were
you may see, 1 Cor. iii. where one was saying, I am
of Paul, another, I am of Apollos, or Cephas, and
he seemed to fear, that this might lead some to build
on another foundation, than that which is laid, Christ
Jesus, but we regard him only as our law-giver, and
therefore are no schismatics, though we cannot submit
to the 20th article of the church of England. This
is again spoken of 1 Cor. xi. 18. where we find, that
divers abuses were crept into their assemblies, and the
women took upon them an undue authority, but, says
he, the head of every woman is the man, and he
likewise commands, 1 Tim. ii. 12. that the woman
shall not usurp authority over the man ; but women
have more than once been supreme heads of the church
of England, endowed with power to make bishops,
and to instruct all the clergy, both in what they
should, and what they should not preach. Queen Elizabeth prohibited all preaching for a time, and she
composed a prayer for the use of her army, so she
might, had she pleased, for her clergy. In the reign
of queen Anne, Mr. Whiston, having published a
book concerning the trinity; all the bishops and clergy met in convocation, addressed the queen, setting
forth, that he had advanced several damnable and
blasphemous assertions, against the doctrine and worship of the ever blessed trinity ; and, in their censure,
earnestly beseeched all Christians, by the mercies of
Christ, to take heed how they gave ear to those false
doctrines. This being their sense of the matter, one
would think they should have immediately censured it;
but their censure could be of no force, till they had
laid it before the queen ; and, upon her majesty's opinion it entirely depended, whether these doctrines,
which the body of the clergy considered as damnable
and blasphemous, were to be rejected by the church
of England as erroneous. Her majesty was of a different

ferent opinion : So her fingle opinion, reader, are you
not furprifed ? her fingle opinion had more weight, than
that of all the bifhops and clergy, thofe fucceffors of the
apoftles, and ambaffadors of Chrift. A fallible woman reftrained the whole body of the clergy in the
moft important part of their office, the keeping out
thofe damnable doctrines, which they prayed the people, by the mercies of Chrift, to beware of. This
needs no comment, it is hiftorical fact. 'Tis from
the reigning king or queen proceeds all power, ecclefiaftical as well as civil. The foveieign may make
more bifhops, as did Henry VII'. he may diffolve a
bifhopric, as Edward VI. did that of Durham: had
not bloooy Mary came to the throne foon after, that
rich fee might have been utterly loft : He may keep
the fees vacant for as many years as he pleafed, as did
queen Elizabeth, by which means the whole conftitution of the church might, in a courfe of years, be
overturned. He may deprive bifhops who will not
fubmit to the laws made by the parliament, as queen
Elizabeth did fourteen at once for oppofing the reformation which fhe and her parliament were pleafes to make
in the church, and as king William did feven, for not
owning him to be king. In fhort, all the clergy together cannot make the leaft alteration in the church,
but the king and parliament can do as they pleafe,
though all the clergy fhould oppofe it. They have
boafted of a divine alliance between church and ftate,
but the former is entirely fubject to the latter ; we
hear, indeed, of the lords fpiritual and temporal, but
an act is as valid when there is not a bifhop upon the
bench, as if the whole twenty fix were there, fo that
they are no neceffary part of the conftitution, as they
would fain be fuppofed.

The church of England differs widely from the
church of Chrift, fo that we may feparate from one,
and ftill remain members of the other. The church
of Chrift is a religious eftablifhment, founded upon
fcripture ; the church of England is a civil eftablifhment, founded upon acts of parliament. Into the
church of Chrift any perfon may be admitted, who
fubmits to the terms appointed by Chrift ; but into
the

the church of England, he cannot be admitted without submitting, besides these, to such as human authority has devised. In the scriptural church of Christ, there are no such officers ever heard of as arch-bishops, deans, arch-deacons, chancellors, &c. in the church of England these are officers of great influence, and high rank. I might add more instances, but one shall suffice. If we enquire after the frame and constitution of the church of Christ, we must look for it only in the bible; but if we enquire after the constitution and frame of the church of England, we must look for it in the statute books, canons, common prayer book, and in the codes of the English law. In whatever the church of England agrees with the church of Christ, we will readily join with it; but since, in some things they differ, we may be true members of the latter, and yet have nothing to do with the former. Had not the clergy themselves been sensible of some such difference, they would never have made such outcries as they have heretofore, about the danger of their church, since Christ hath promised nothing shall ever prevail against his, Mat. xvi. 18. Some will tell us, that these things concern ministers only, but the laity have nothing to do with them; this is priestcraft outright. The laity are as much interested in the truths of the gospel, as much obliged to defend them, and as much intitled to the rewards therein promised, as the greatest prelate in the land. The laity must give an account to Christ, how far they have regarded his honour, and those who submit to any unscriptural impositions, when they are persuaded of their being such; or who will not examine into the grounds of them, are full as inexcusable as the imposers. But it has been the fault of the people, as that strenuous advocate for the church, the learned and pious Mr. Hales observes, ' that through ' sloth and blind obedience, they examined, not the ' things they were taught, but, like beasts of burden, ' patiently couched down, and indifferently under- ' went, whatever their superiors laid on them.' How great this load is, popish countries testify. Italy, the garden of the world, by submitting to the power of priests, is rendered despicable and wretched : The

power

power of the clergy feemed to be rifing to an infup-
portable height in this country fince the reformation,
for archbifhop Laud had the impudence to declare, he
hoped to fee the time, when no jack gentleman in the
kingdom fhould be fuffered to wear his hat before the
meaneft prieft. Our pious forefathers did indeed make
a diftinction, between minifterial and lay conformity,
but when their oppreffions were too great to be born,
to the honour of the laity be it fpoken, when their
minifters were ejected, fined, imprifoned, banifhed,
they did not defert, but fupported and fhared with
them in all their troubles. The fame noble fpirit
ftill fubfifts in many, they will not fubmit to the authority of the church, and fupport thofe honeft men
who cannot comply with them, by an attendance on
their preaching, and the affiftance of their purfes.
That many are grown indifferent to this great caufe
of religious liberty, is, in general, either owing to
an indifference to all religion, or not duly confidering
the matter. Unlefs the laity look to it, the clergy
will foon triumph, unlefs they ftir in a reformation, it
will never come from priefts, who are always ready to
cry out, the church, that is, their power and revenues
are in danger. Without the laity, Chriftianity would
never have fpread, popery never have been fuppreffed,
nor pure religion been recovered from popifh darknefs.
Many of the clergy of all forts have been ornaments
to human nature, and laid down their lives for the
gofpel, but it was their brethren who thus ufed them,
or ftirred up the people to do it. A pious, humble
minifter is intitled to honour and efteem ; a carelefs,
haughty one, to contempt, of whatever party he is.
It is to the laity this apoftolic charge is delivered,
Rom. xvi. 17. to mark, (i. e. to obferve carefully)
them that caufe divifions and offences contrary to the
chriftian doctrine, and to avoid them. Now, thofe
who fet up ceremonies of human invention, and com-
mand the fubjects of Chrift to fubmit to them,
or refufe to admit fuch to their communion as will
not fubmit to fuch rights, reafon will tell us,
are the men that caufe divifions and offences contrary
to the Chriftian doctrine, and fuch the laity are exprefly

prefly commanded by the apoftle to avoid. If any prieft tells a layman it is his duty to fubmit to what the fathers of the church teach, he fhould tell him, he will fubmit to none but Chrift; that laymen are as much concerned for the honour of Chrift, and the religion of the bible, equally interefted in it, equally obliged to defend it as any prieft whatever.

As to the infamous principles of conforming to the religion of the country where we dwell, I hope the reader will fcorn it, fince this will lead a man to be a prefbyterian in Scotland, a papift in France, a mahometan in Turkey, and in India a worfhipper of the devil. If we are Chriftians, let us, like the noble Bereans fearch the fcriptures; if we are reafonable beings, let us not be flaves to cuftom, but votaries of truth. Let us agree to eftablifhments, as far and no farther than they agree with thefe. Religion is a thing of too great importance to change and vary with cuftoms and climates.

Thus have I reprefented the principles of our diffent fairly and impartially. If any one fhould think me too warm, it is the caufe which warms me; for I may prefume to fay, that the honour of my Redeemer, and the purity of his religion, lie near my heart; where thefe are concerned, lukewarmnefs is criminal. I fincerely wifh this little work may ftir up a fpirit of enquiry among proteftant diffenters, and any others who may happen to perufe it. Thofe who have time for reading, will gain much knowledge both in civil and religious affairs, from Mr. Neal's Hiftory of the Puritans, an excellent work, drawn up with fo much care, that after his adverfaries had faid every thing againft it they could invent, their objections were fo trifling as to do real honour to it, fince fo large a work contained fo few faults. But as fome may not have leifure to perufe this, the Memoirs of the Reformation, by the pious Mr Benjamin Bennet, or the Hiftory of the Nonconformifts, prefixed to Mr. Pearce's excellent vindication of the Diffenters, one or another of thefe may be eafily procured, and read with great improvement. Mr. Pearce's work is dedicated to the minifters of the church of Scotland; but though we efteem them as,
coming

coming nearer in their form of government to the simplicity of the gospel, than the church of England, yet as they impose some other things as necessary besides the scriptures, we cannot agree entirely with them, and few dissenters, who understand their principles, would join with them now, though our forefathers held them in higher estimation. But a book which I could wish to see in the hands of every dissenter, and would recommend to any who are desirous of a larger acquaintance with our principles, is, The Dissenting Gentleman's Letters to Mr. White, edit. 4. duod. price 3s. 6d.

This may well be called an unanswerable performance, as long as the bible is the rule of controversy, and is writ in so lively and spirited a manner, that it cannot fail of giving pleasure, nor can a lover of religious liberty read it without rapture. I suppose no one will think it worth their while to take notice of this little pamphlet; however, if this should be the case, I would advise them first to read and answer that piece. I have frequently used his expressions, and those who read it will not blame me, since they will see it is impossible to find better. The author of that piece, a venerable minister of the West, scarcely knows me even by name, nor I him so much as by sight; so that it cannot be partiality to the man, but a regard for the work, that makes me recommend it thus earnestly.

I would humbly offer a few things to the consideration of protestant dissenters. If our interest is so important, ought we not to unite all our strength to support it? It grieves me when I hear of congregations being divided, divisions soon brings on destruction, and many flourishing congregations have been ruined by it. A bold, factious man, whom all the congregation ought to avoid as a disturber of its peace, has sometimes such influence as to make a minister's situation uneasy, and cause such breaches as will never be healed. This has been particularly the case on choosing a new minister, some are resolved to have their own humours gratified, how much soever the rest of the people are disgusted, and would sooner see them divided, than agree in the election of one who is not exactly suited to their taste. This is not acting with a Christian spirit, we ought to bear with the weak-
nesses

nesses and infirmities of others, as well as to please our-
selves. Whoever is attached to any particular sentiments, should consider that others have their prejudices
too, that we ought therefore to bear and forbear.
When any one votes in the choice of a minister, let him
consider, that he is to teach others, as well as himself,
and therefore they ought to be gratified ; else the great
work of turning sinners from the errors of their ways,
and building up the saints in their most holy faith,
the great design of preaching can go on but slowly,
where the preacher is not generally approved. If any
one thinks him not to be entirely in his sentiments, it
ought to be considered, that ministers have an equal
right with others to think and judge for themselves ;
that the best and wisest men have in some things differed,
and that the improvement of the whole society should
be preferred to the pleasure of two or three persons.
Were we always influenced by such considerations, on
these occasions, the unhappy divisions would never have
happened, which have so much hurt our common cause.
May these thoughts be laid to heart, and societies instead of dividing, lay aside their prejudices, and begin
to unite, so that instead of two congregations in a town,
distinguished by odious party names, we may see one
united in love, and the bonds of christian charity. Why
should differences in opinion so much divide us ? Let
ministers confine themselves to scripture language, and
adhere strictly to the plainer and more important
doctrines of the gospel, then we shall again flourish and
revive. For what reason the baptists and presbyterians
should be divided in any town, I cannot conceive,
where they agree in most other points. Unless the
congregations are large, one minister may serve for
both, and another be procured to administer the ordinances of baptism in their respective methods ; or they
may have two ministers, only leaving all disputes out of the
pulpits on the Lord's day, and if they cannot do without
them, let there be a lecture some day in the week on purpose. Such a union would evidence a true Christian spirit,
and by this means many small congregations in the
neighbourhood may be supplied, which are now destitute ;
for when instead of two all meet in the same place, one
of

of the ministers might be spared to assist those who could not of themselves maintain one; this would be doing service to our common interest, supporting religious liberty, and scripture Christianity, without any human inventions, the principles we all profess, and which are of much greater consequence than those which divide us. This would likewise help to add to the income, which is now frequently so small.

Another matter worthy of confideration is this, there are many congregations which cannot or do not raise more than thirty or forty pounds per annum, the most either of these sums can do is to maintain a single man, and hardly that, as ministers are expected to appear, without great frugality; but all know how very insufficient such a falary is to support a family, utterly impossible, where there is a large one. Now would it not be very right, when two such congregations are fituated within feven, eight, or even twelve miles of each other, to content themfelves with one minister, who shall preach to them alternately, and the other Sunday some grave, worthy perfon read a fermon to the people, and if he does not chufe to pray extempore, excellent forms are at hand. Those who confider our prefent circumftances, may fee that this would be a very ufeful method of proceeding, and I doubt not that every fociety affords one at leaft-capable of carrying on fuch a fervice with decency and credit. It fhould be the care of fuch not to grow conceited, and as for any ridicule this might expofe them to, it would be beneath the notice of a wife and good man, defirous of promoting, to the utmoft of his power, the intereft of the Redeemer. Wit and humour will foon die away, but thofe who have been any way inftrumental in promoting the great caufe of religion, whether regularly bred to the miniftry, or not, will be entitled to the glorious promife, Dan. xii. 3. of fhining as the brightnefs of the firmament, and as the ftars for ever and ever. By this means the worfhip of God might be carried on in a very profitable manner to every ferious hearer, and minifters would have a more comfortable maintainance; whereas at prefent the profpect is fo difcouraging, that perfons are unwilling to bring up

F   their

their children to that office, many fo brought up are
obliged to leave it for fome other profeffion, and numbers of excellent worthy men, ftruggle with fuch diffi-
culties as humanity cannot think of without a tear.
One of the congregations would certainly be under the
difadvantage of not having the minifter refident among
them, but he might take opportunities to vifit that people, by coming to them on the Saturday morning, or
ftaying till Monday night. If fome fuch method is
not adopted, many congregations will foon be without
minifters; whereas on this plan, encouragement would
be given to young men to fit themfelves for the office;
and when God fees his people fo concerned for the
purity of religion, he will raife them up paftors after
his own heart. In fome towns there may be a large
and rich congregation, and a poor one in the neighbourhood; two minifters might preach at them alternately, and the larger congregation give fome affiftance
to the paftor of the poor one, though not to make him
equal to their own. Minifters who know what pains
muft be taken, efpecially by young men, to prepare two
fermons every week, will not object to this regulation,
if agreeable to the people, who generally love fome
variety, and it would be a means of eafing both. Many
think that the office of a minifter is a very eafy one,
but making two fermons every week (which unlefs a
minifter does he finks into contempt, except the people
will be contented with his old ones one part of the day,
which fome do not like) is to moft very hard work indeed, too much for fome to bear, and has haftened the
death of many excellent men. If then a minifter fhould
upon a chance give another's fermon, it is very unreafonable to raife an outcry about it, and account him a
lazy preacher.

The importance of our diffent fhould likewife lead
us to be generous in the fupport of it. Many are fo,
but others fo far from doing what they can, do not
what they ought. Our pious anceftors, notwithftanding
their fevere loffes, were at great expence in building
thofe places which their pofterity will fcarce repair, and
rifked their all in fupport of that to which a little is now
applied with grudging. The middle fort of people in
trade

rade are generally thought to be the moſt generous. Many of them with a few hundreds in trade, which is very uncertain, will ſubſcribe near as much, and ſome-:imes more than thoſe who have as many hundreds :very year, and that too in eſtates, which run not half :he riſk ; ſurely this betrays great indifference to the :auſe. The poorer ſort might contribute ſomething, and even ſixpence per quarter, were there are many, might amount to ſomething handſome, if all gave ac-cording to their circumſtances, which every one knows beſt himſelf, there would be leſs reaſon for complaint. Many ſocieties in our great towns are certainly capable of aſſiſting others, as well as ſupporting themſelves. The diſſenters in London, to their honour be it ſpoken, have done great things ; their example has been fol-lowed in ſome places, though not in many, where there is ſufficient ability. This cannot be ſo much imputed to a want of zeal, as of conſideraton, was ſuch a thing ſet on foot, by ſome active perſon, in every ſuch town, it would be ſupported by others; that congre-gations in the country are by no means backward in occaſional collections is evident from the large ſums raiſed in them for America ; but conſidering our own circumſtances at home, great prudence ſhould be uſed in encouraging their applications. If on the Lord's day neareſt Bartholomew day, when ſo many of our worthy mi niſters were forcibly ejected, a ſermon was preached on the principles of our diſſent, it would be very uſeful to the young people ; and after that a collection was made in covered boxes, ſo that every perſon might be at liberty to put in what they chuſe, without its being known how much, or how little ; it would be a great help to the London funds, now much burthened, whe-ther it was ſent up to them, or diſtributed in the country, as the ſocieties ſaw fit. It is to be hoped ſome who truly regard the cauſe, will ſet forward this good work.

The rich and faſhionable, eſpecially where the in-tereſt is low, are apt to forſake the cauſe, but certainly thoſe who leave the diſſenters, merely becauſe going to the eſtabliſhed church is more faſhionable, would on the ſame principles throw off Chriſtianity itſelf in a

heathen

heathen country. Those who found their religion in reason and scripture, will not be indifferent to what society they join themselves, but attend where they can be best improved, and the rules of the gospel are most strictly observed; you that are guided in the great affairs of religion by fashion, be not deceived, for really you have no religion at all. Others, Demas like, have forsaken us when they have grown rich; if we enquire after such persons, where shall we find them? The established church does not encrease, though we decrease. It has been often and truly observed, that when men leave the dissenters, they too often throw off that strictness and sobriety which are essential to a true Christian, and go into that luxury, vanity, and disregard to religion, which it is to be feared will ruin the nation. This is not uncharitable; it is fact; I write it with reluctance and grief.

Let not the young be disheartened, because those who know nothing about the matter, may sometimes ridicule them; "Whosoever shall be ashamed of me, "and of my words, (says Christ, before this sinful and "adulterous generation) of him also will I be ashamed "before my Father, who is in heaven," Matt. x. 33. Remember that the Christians once were a sect every where spoken against, Acts xxviii. 22. And let those who have hitherto been faithful, resolve to maintain that religion and worship to their latest breath, which they esteem most pure and scriptural, and they shall not lose their reward.

And may all of us by a conduct and behaviour becoming the gospel, adorn the doctrine of God our Saviour in all things, for an attachment to the purest church, without real holiness of life, will only expose us to the contempt of mankind, and a severer judgment at the great day.

I have not put my name to this address, it is needless, that would recommend it to no one, but the importance of the subject merits the attention of every person. I have only to beg, that it may not be slightly run over, and then thrown aside, but that those who approve the design, would distribute it among their friends, and the poorer sort of dissenters, that so our
religion

religion being founded in knowledge, we may be no longer wavering and inconftant, but grounded and fettled. Much time has been employed about this fmall work ; fhould it however in any degree anfwer the end propofed, it will give me a pleafure not to be defcribed. To the ferious perufal of every proteftant diffenter, and to the blefling of God I commit it.

POST-

POSTCRIPT.

Diffenting minifters accepting the title of doctor of divinity, has been charged upon them lately as an inconfiftency, and a mark of their fondnefs for honorary diftinctions as well as others. If we take the title doctor of divinity in its literal fenfe, it means no more than teacher of divinity, and is therefore lefs refpectful than mafter, a common form of addrefs to all men, but as it is always accounted a diftinguifhing title, it muft be remembered it is not conferred on them as divines, but as the reward of literary merit, and fo far no diffenter ever oppofed any titles. The late Dr. Harris had made himfelf known as an hiftorian; a univerfity thought proper to fhew their refpect to him, and as he was a divine, beftowed that upon him which his labours in hiftory had obtained, and the cafe is the fame with others, they pretend to no high claims, no additional powers, no peculiar diftinction above their brethren in the miniftry on this account, or give the leaft approbation to the members of that church who beftow it, but continue the fame in every refpect as minifters, and receive this merely as a reward of their knowledge in hiftory, philofophy or any other fcience as well as divinity. But bifhops, as bifhops claim an equal title with the peers of the realm, and the archbifhop precedes all except the blood royal, they make a part in the great councils of the nation, are highly exalted above all the heads of the clergy, cloath themfelves in purple, ride in chariots, all fupported at the church's expence, and to look as much as poffible like royalty, call their houfes palaces, which no nobleman whatever, in the kingdom does that I ever heard of. The degree of D. D. in the church, likewife qualifies a man to hold two or more livings, how abfurd is it then to reflect on our minifters for taking fuch degrees, as if there was any refemblance between us and them.

However fuppofing we are wrong, does this alter the cafe? Will one man's fault excufe, much lefs juftify another in committing the fame. If it is wrong to ac-

cept

cept of fuch diftinctions, why does not the church decline them? If there is no impropriety in them, why
is it objected to us? Let the cafe be as it will, it at
moft only affects fome few; thus diftinguifhed, our
caufe as diffenters will ftand good, independant of all
the doctors in the world; but the civil powers of the
bifhops are faid to be interwoven into the very conftitution, and upon the exercife of their pretended fpiritual ones, depends the very exiftence of the church, a
regular miniftry and valid ordinances. The title of reverend is alfo beftowed upon us, but then not claimed
by a few but given to all indifferently; we have no
right reverend father in God to exalt fome above their
brethren, as the laity are pleafed to fhew this mark of
refpect to the profeffion, why may it not be accepted
as well as that of mafter or fir? fhould any minifter
however, fhow any mark of diflike at not being fo ad-
dreffed, his weaknefs and folly would expofe him to
pity and contempt?

F I N I S.

www.ingramcontent.com/pod-product-compliance
Lightning Source LLC
Chambersburg PA
CBHW032044090426
42733CB00030B/650